Contents

Preface

House quilts have always been my favorite quilts. The first quilt block that I ever stitched was a colorful House on a Hill, embellished with embroidered shrubs, flowers and architectural details. I find myself returning to this favorite theme and have made many variations of house quilts since this first endeavor.

At one point in my life, I wanted to be an architect. I constantly sketched house plans, arranging rooms in the most convenient manner. I still fill my leisure hours touring new homes and sketching the plans, adding my own creative variations. Combining rooms effectively, yet creatively, in an efficient manner to achieve an integrated house is very much like combining blocks, lattices and borders into a quilt.

I collect pottery, needlework and folk art with a house theme. So with my preoccupation with houses and house quilts, it seemed appropriate to choose House on a Hill as a logo for That Patchwork Place.

But house quilts have a charm that speaks to many quilters. Perhaps the warmth given by the suggestions of "hearth and home" provides more than physical comfort. A sense of order prevails in a house quilt as each house block stands in neat rows, separated from its neighbor by an appropriate border, offering a comforting contrast to the frantic upheaval of daily life.

The most popular house quilt has been the Schoolhouse. *Quilters Newsletter Magazine*[1] explored this in a recent article.

"...As the Industrial Revolution took hold of America there were so many changes in lifestyle and ideas that Americans began to feel nostalgic about their past, wishing for a return to the good old days. From the 1870's until the turn of the century quilt designs became notably realistic as quilters tried to portray the things around them in cloth. People, household implements, and buildings were among the popular items cut from fabric. The favorite of these, and the pattern with the most variations, was what we today call Little Red Schoolhouse, or just House Quilt. The rest of the realistic designs of this period have more or less faded from memory, but House Quilt variations have never lost their appeal. Today the Little Red Schoolhouse is considered an American classic.

"Ruth Finley, in her 1929 book *Old Patchwork Quilts and the Women Who Made Them*, shows a Little Red Schoolhouse quilt and suggests that the popular pattern may have originated in New Jersey during the 1870's. The Orlofskys *(Quilts in America)* discovered an Album House Quilt in New Jersey, dating from the third quarter of the nineteenth century, with a nameplate on each door for the maker of the quilt block. Dolores Hinson's *Quilting Manual* shows yet another Little Red School House from the same period. The 1893 Ladies Art Company Catalog, *Diagrams of Quilt, Sofa and Pin Cushion Patterns*, included at least three variations of house patterns, among them Little Red House..."

Several house quilts were featured in the East Bay Heritage Quilters' show, *Quilts, A Tradition of Variations*.[2]

"The popularity of the Schoolhouse quilt can be attributed to the push by the federal government in the late nineteenth and early twentieth centuries to educate Americans. One of the early respected positions available to single women was that of school teacher in the one-room schoolhouses of the midwest and plains states. Many eastern women were educated at Normal Schools and then pioneered sparsely populated areas. The democratic dream of free education for all was becoming a reality."

House quilts can also be a representational mapping of a community in cloth. A quilter organizes the houses into rows, in much the same manner as houses are built on streets. Some house quilts include other structures, such as churches or barns. These quilts illustrate history in cloth, expressing the way in which women regard their neighborhood or community.

1. *Quilters Newsletter Magazine*, (September, 1983), pp. 28-29.
2. *Quilts, A Tradition of Variations*, (Albany, California: East Bay Heritage Quilters, 1982) opposite plate 49.

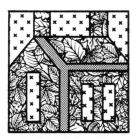

Little Red Schoolhouse

Album House Quilt

Little Red School House

Little Red House

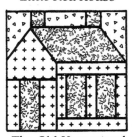

The Old Homestead

Introduction

Housing Projects contains templates for 10 variations of house blocks. Directions are given for using these blocks to make 15 quilts of various sizes and for 12 small projects which use only a single block or two blocks.

There are four sections in this book. The first is a series of brief introductory guidelines to use when planning a project. While directions are given for the construction of a specific quilt or project, it is hoped that you will combine the blocks, settings and borders to personalize a project and design your own quilt.

The second section of this book contains patterns and directions for house quilts. Included with each pattern are full-size templates and piecing diagrams.

Complete directions for 12 small projects comprise the third section of this book. These small projects are excellent for beginners and also offer a use for "trial blocks" or other "false starts." Perhaps the color scheme of a House on a Hill block was not exactly right for your quilt, but it might make a lovely apron bib, tote or album cover.

The last section is a reference section on quilt construction, written by Marsha McCloskey. It includes information on tools and materials, templates, cutting, machine piecing and quilt assembly. Enough guidance is given for a beginner to successfully complete each project. Experienced stitchers may feel more comfortable with their own sewing methods.

Planning Your Project

Fabric Selection

I recommend purchasing 100% cotton fabrics. It is the easiest fabric to work with and there are many prints available. A polyester blend fabric will be more difficult to use and is more susceptible to "bearding" when it is used with a polyester batting. "Bearding" or batting migration is caused when the fibers of the polyester batting work their way through the polyester fabric. It is not as likely to occur when 100% cotton fabric is used.

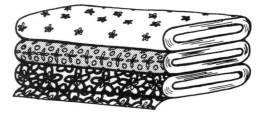

Preparing Fabrics

Wash all fabrics first to preshrink and test for colorfastness. Continue to wash fabric until the rinse water is completely clear. Add a square of white fabric to each washing of the fabric. When this white fabric remains its original color, the fabric is colorfast. A cupful of vinegar in the rinse water may also be used to help set difficult dyes.

Do not use any fabric of which you are uncertain. Many people avoid prewashing their fabric because they prefer to work on "fresh fabric" or because they plan to have the item dry-cleaned. These people should be prepared for the possibility that the colors in the fabric may run if they accidentally become wet. Color dyes are also apt to rub off.

Color

Color will influence a finished project's appearance more than any other factor. The time used in selecting the fabrics for your project will be well spent.

Choose prints with an eye for color and variety. For more "eye appeal," vary the scale of the prints. (Don't use all tiny flowered calicoes.) More interest is created when you add a print that is larger in scale or has wider spaces between the designs.

Choose a background fabric carefully. Many quilt patterns have relatively large unpieced areas as background to pieced designs. These areas are generally light in color while the design motif is dark. Good background prints for such designs have subtle allover texture, fine detail and movement without being spotty or linear.

Color schemes are influenced by the project or quilt that you are making. Feminine or baby items lend themselves to pastel colors. They can often be enhanced by ruffled eyelet, laces, trims or ribbons. For masculine items, use earthy colors and fabrics with interesting textures such as corduroy or denim.

You may choose solid colors to take advantage of the strong graphic design that can be achieved with a house quilt. Combining a strong color such as navy or red with muslin is a favorite color scheme. Alternate muslin blocks serve as good backgrounds for quilting designs. Rainbow effects, shocking contrasts or subtle color variances can all be created with solid color fabrics. Using polished cottons, velvets or denims in solid colors will add much textural interest.

Do keep in mind that a strong solid color or dark print will make the houses appear larger than if a medium range print is used. This can be seen in the Schoolhouse quilt on page 47. You may want to compensate for this by selecting a 10" or smaller block, or by increasing the lattice width to at least 3 1/2" if you are using a 12" block.

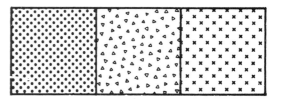

*Poor combination
(similar scale and density)*

*Good combination
(varies in density, scale and print)*

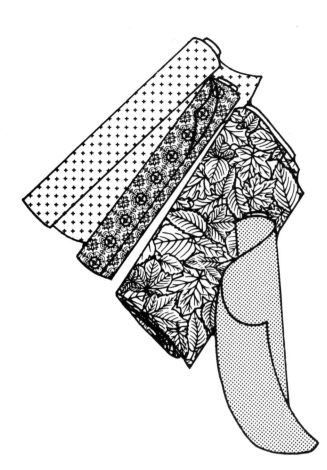

House quilts make excellent "scrap quilts" since most of the pieces are small and can utilize leftover pieces of fabric. Each house, roof and grass area can be made from a different fabric. Do make sure that the fabrics all have the same color intensity. Try to work in ranges of colors restricted to subdued or greyed colors, brights or perhaps pastels.

Since repetition is an important element in quilt design, it is wise to repeat one or two fabrics in every block. The strippy sampler quilt shown on the back cover repeats the same pink fabric for chimneys and the green fabric for grass in every block. In addition, the same small print is used in varying pastel colors for the houses, and a similar geometric print in deeper tones is used for all the roofs.

The School House quilt pattern on page 39 lends itself to a scrap quilt. If the left segment of the block is done in a darker shade of color than the right segment, it gives the illusion that the sun is shading this portion of the house. All the houses do not need to be identical, but they all should feature darker and lighter shades of a color.

You may let nature help you select the color scheme for a house quilt by choosing a blue sky, green grass, white house, red chimneys, and so on. The Cabin in the Country quilt, shown in Plate 11 on page 45, effectively uses a pale blue print which suggests swirling snow on a winter day. The forest green trees, which have been strip pieced, offer a perfect contrast as they frame the houses.

Study the color photographs in this book and read the color selection tips included with each quilt to help you choose a color scheme. Arrange fabric selections next to each other (including some that you're not sure of) and look at the fabrics every time you pass. Do this for several days, pausing to eliminate, rearrange or add other fabrics. When you feel comfortable with the fabric selections, it's time to begin the project.

Fabric Requirements

With each of the 15 house quilts in this book, fabric requirements are given to make the quilt in a specific size. If you vary the quilt size, you will need to compute the amount of fabric needed for your individualized project.

Blocks: Consult the Materials section for the quilt block you are making to determine the number of fabrics needed. Make the necessary templates for this quilt block. Place the templates to be cut from a specified fabric on a 45" piece of muslin. Determine the yardage needed for one block and multiply that figure by the number of blocks in the quilt. Repeat this process for each fabric that is required.

Lattices and Borders: Measure the longest lattice or border strip. longer than 44", and you do not wish to piece these borders, bu enough yardage to accommodate the length. Extra yardage ca usually be cut into bias strips and used to bind the quilt.

Backing: If a quilt or wall hanging is less than 42" wide, simpl measure the length of the quilt and purchase yardage in tha amount. If a quilt or wall hanging is more than 42" wide, you w need to piece the backing. Purchase twice the quilt width and sea together as shown.

Excess yardage from backing can also be cut into bias strips a used to bind the quilt.

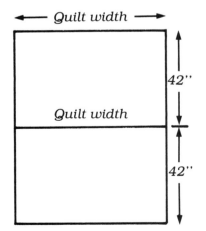

Seam together fabric for quilt backing.

Quilt Size

You may wish to adjust the size of some of the design ideas, changing them from wall hangings to bed quilts or vice versa. My personal feeling is that the emphatic visual statement of any house quilt is better suited for a wall hanging than a bed cover. It is a design that appears best when viewed "straight on" in its entirety rather than draped over a bed. Nevertheless, the following information should prove helpful.

Mattress size: Twin: 39" x 75"
                 Double: 52" x 75"
                 Queen: 60" x 80"
                 King: 72" x 84"

To determine the finished size of a bed quilt, add 10" for a pillow tuck and allow a 10" to 12" drop on three sides to cover the mattress. Or you may choose to make the standard sizes of commercially produced comforters, designed to be used with a dust ruffle:

     Twin: 68" x 86"
     Double: 76" x 86"
     Queen: 86" x 86"
     King: 101" x 86"

To determine the number of blocks needed, divide the length and width of the quilt desired by the size of the blocks.

     Example: 72" x 84" = 6 x 7 rows of 12" blocks.

If you desire to add borders or lattice, subtract a block from each row and divide this measurement into lattice strips.

Example: 72" x 86" = 5 x 6 rows of 12" blocks with 2" lattice strips between blocks and as a border.

You can decrease the number of blocks even further by increasing the number and size of the borders.

I have resolved this size dilemma by making most of my quilts one standard size which I find quite versatile. A quilt approximately 80" square will work as a coverlet on both double and queen size mattresses. I fill in the uncovered area near the headboard with an assortment of pillow shams and small pillows. In addition, this size quilt can easily be hung on a wall in most homes or used as a table cover over a floor-length cloth on a round table.

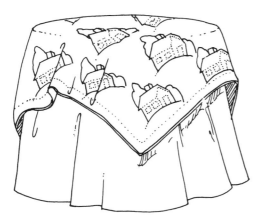

Quilt used as table cover over a floor-length cloth

Coverlet, 80" square

Quilt Design

Blocks

All of the quilts in this book are made up of repeated house designs called unit blocks. Some quilts alternate the unit blocks with unpieced blocks or with two different unit blocks such as Cabin Raising, which combines the House and Log Cabin blocks. Choose a block and experiment with setting plans to design your own quilt. Most of the blocks will work well in various sets.

Setting Plans

When unit blocks are sewn together to make a quilt top, it is called "the set." Most house blocks cannot be set together side by side, but require separation by unpieced blocks or lattice strips. Since the house blocks are representational and have a definite top and bottom, they are usually set "straight on" rather than diagonally. Study the following setting plans and substitute the house block of your choice.

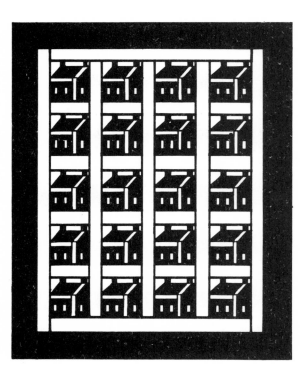

Plan A: House Blocks Set with Lattice Strips

This is the most common way to "set" a house block, since it effectively separates the houses. If the lattice strips are the same as the background color of the block, as in the Schoolhouse quilt on page 47 and the House quilt in Plate 4 on page 42, the houses will be emphasized. Lattice squares may be used in addition to lattice strips to frame the house blocks, as shown in Plate 1 on page 41.

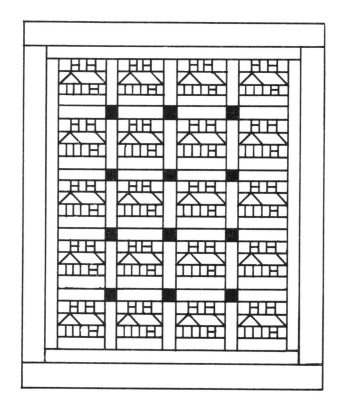

10

Plan B: Alternating Blocks

Combining two different quilt blocks can form a strong overall design used to frame the house blocks. Both Nine Patch and Double Irish Chain work well here. (Four extra squares of the Double Irish Chain must be pieced to the adjacent house blocks.) Note that an odd number of blocks are again used in the rows and columns. If the house blocks are used in the corners rather than the alternating block, the quilt will have a different emphasis.

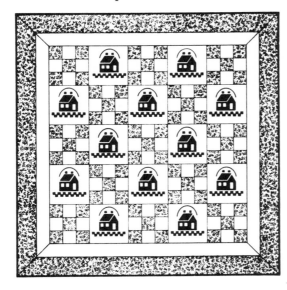

Plan C: Alternating Blocks with a Barnraising Variation

The word "Barnraising" is used to describe a set that radiates concentrically from the center of a quilt. The first diagram shows Log Cabin blocks with their dark and light sides arranged to frame eight house blocks. An even number of blocks must be used in the rows and columns to achieve this arrangement.[3] A Barnraising design can also be achieved using Schoolhouse and pieced triangle blocks. In this design, an odd number of blocks has been used and the houses have been set to face different directions.

Schoolhouse blocks set with pieced triangle blocks

House blocks set with Log Cabin blocks

3. *This type of set is referred to as Barnraising because it reminded early quilters of the arrangement of logs and boards used when they gathered to help a neighbor erect a barn.*

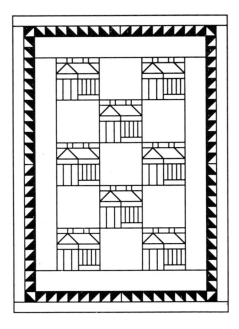

Plan D: House Block and Unpieced Block

Borders are not always necessary with this setting plan. A quilt will look visually in balance if you work with an odd number of blocks in each row and column. This puts a pieced block in each corner of the quilt. The unpieced blocks will allow space to feature a favorite quilting design, or you may quilt an outline of the house pattern used for the pieced block.

Plan E: Half Block Additions

Combining half blocks with unit blocks will add more variety to the quilt design. Cabin in the Country, shown in Plate 11 on page 45, combines tree half blocks with the house blocks. Lattice strips of background fabric are also used to separate the design elements.

Tree blocks are half blocks which add to this house design.

Plan F: Strippy Sets

The setting design used for this type of quilt can be used to make a sampler quilt of house blocks. Each row features a different sized house block with strips of sky and grass added to divide the houses. The house blocks increase in size with the smallest houses at the top, giving an illusion of distance through perspective. The border is optional and was not used with the original strippy quilts popular in the late 1800s.[4]

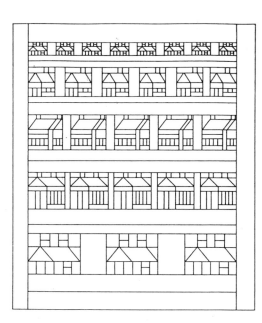

Rows of house blocks combined "strippy style" to form a sampler.

Plan G: Random Sets

House blocks can be appliqued randomly to a background; see Schoolhouse, shown in Plate 16 on page 48. The colors of the background fabric were carefully chosen to represent the land and sky. Stars, railroad tracks and other structures were carefully added. This quilt is a representation of the community in cloth and details the history of the town.

4. *"...This technique describes patchwork that is made up from strips of fabric rather than blocks or repeated shapes. The basic Strippy originated in northeast England and is the simplest type of patchwork made from long lengths of fabric cut to the size of the quilt..." Miche Walker,* **The Pattern Library Quilting and Patchwork,** *(New Yor N.Y.: Ballantine Books, 1983), p. 46.*

Quilts

This section of the book consists of directions and templates for 15 different quilts. Each quilt is identified by the block name and size. All templates for the blocks are labeled with the template number, block name, finished block size and the number of pieces to be cut for one block. Templates for borders and set pieces indicate the number of pieces to cut for the entire quilt.

Cutting directions will sometimes specify that a template be reversed, so that a "mirror image" shape is cut. Cut the first piece with the template face up and then flip it over face down to cut the reversed piece. If you wish to change the direction that a house faces, reverse the templates before cutting.

Reference is also made on each template to the fabric to be used. This is meant to help you identify template pieces and relate them to the finished quilts. Do not let this labeling restrict your design; feel free to substitute your own colorations to achieve more individual results.

Where it is needed, shapes are marked with a grain line. All templates, except those for applique, include 1/4" seam allowances.

Border strips should always be cut from yardage before the templates are cut, ensuring that continuous yardage is available for the border strip. If border strips must be pieced, seams should be pressed open and placed in the center of each side of the quilt for minimum visibility.

Some of the quilts are adapted from antique quilts and have been changed slightly to make them easier to construct. Therefore, they may look different from or be a different size than the quilts shown in the photographs.

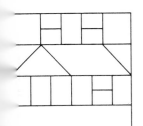
House on a Hill 12"

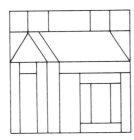
Schoolhouse 12"

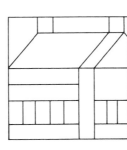
House 12"

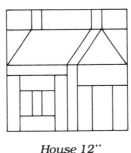
House 12"

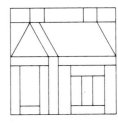
Schoolhouse 11"

House 10"

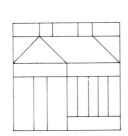
School House 8"

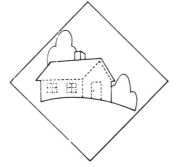
Home Sweet Home 8"

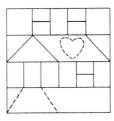
Suzanne's House 6"

Little Love Nest 4"

House on a Hill

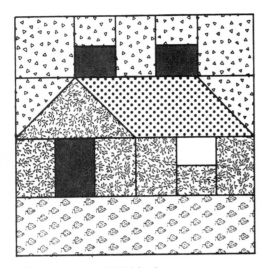

12" House on a Hill block

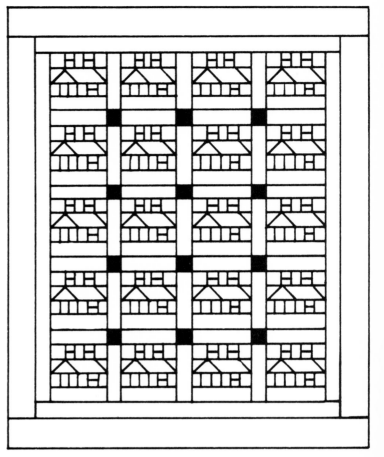

House on a Hill Quilt 74" x 89"

Color:

Let nature help select a color scheme as you plan a house quilt. A checked house with a blue door, red chimneys and a yellow window looks charming. Combine with green grass and blue sky. A very muted color scheme of blues and beige was selected for the quilt made from this pattern, shown on page 41.

Dimensions: 74" x 89"

Measurements for borders and pattern pieces include 1/4" seam allowances.

Materials: 45"-wide fabric

1 1/4 yds. fabric for house pieces
1/2 yd. fabric for roof
3/8 yd. fabric for chimneys and door
1/8 yd. fabric for window
1 1/4 yds. fabric for sky
3/4 yd. fabric for grass
2 1/4 yds. dark background fabric for lattice
  squares, border and bias binding
2 1/8 yds. medium print fabric for lattice and first
  border
5 yds. fabric for backing
81" x 96" Mountain Mist® batting

Directions:

1. This quilt has simple borders with straight sewn corners. From medium print, cut two 3 1/2" x 72 1/2" strips for length and two 3 1/2" x 63 1/2" strips for width. For the second border, cut two 5 3/4" x 78 1/2" strips for length and two 5 3/4" x 74" strips for width from dark background fabric.
2. Cut 31 lattice strips 3 1/2" x 12 1/2" and 12 lattice squares 3 1/2" x 3 1/2".
3. Cut and piece 20 House on a Hill blocks.
4. Set pieced blocks together with 3 1/2" x 12 1/2" lattice strips. Piece four rows of lattice strips and lattice squares. Join rows of pieced blocks and lattice strips together for quilt top.
5. Add straight sewn borders.
6. Add backing and batting, then quilt or tie. Suggested quilting design: Quilt house blocks 1/4" away from each seam. Quilt a 3" grid through lattice blocks, lattice strips and border.
7. Bind with fabric to match border.

14

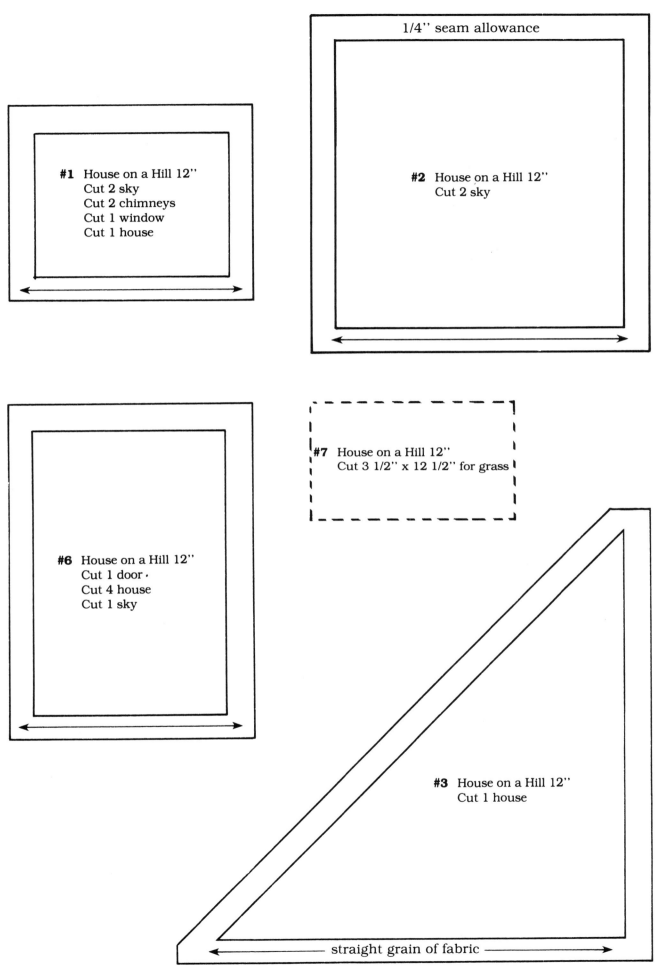

#1 House on a Hill 12"
Cut 2 sky
Cut 2 chimneys
Cut 1 window
Cut 1 house

1/4" seam allowance

#2 House on a Hill 12"
Cut 2 sky

#7 House on a Hill 12"
Cut 3 1/2" x 12 1/2" for grass

#6 House on a Hill 12"
Cut 1 door
Cut 4 house
Cut 1 sky

#3 House on a Hill 12"
Cut 1 house

straight grain of fabric

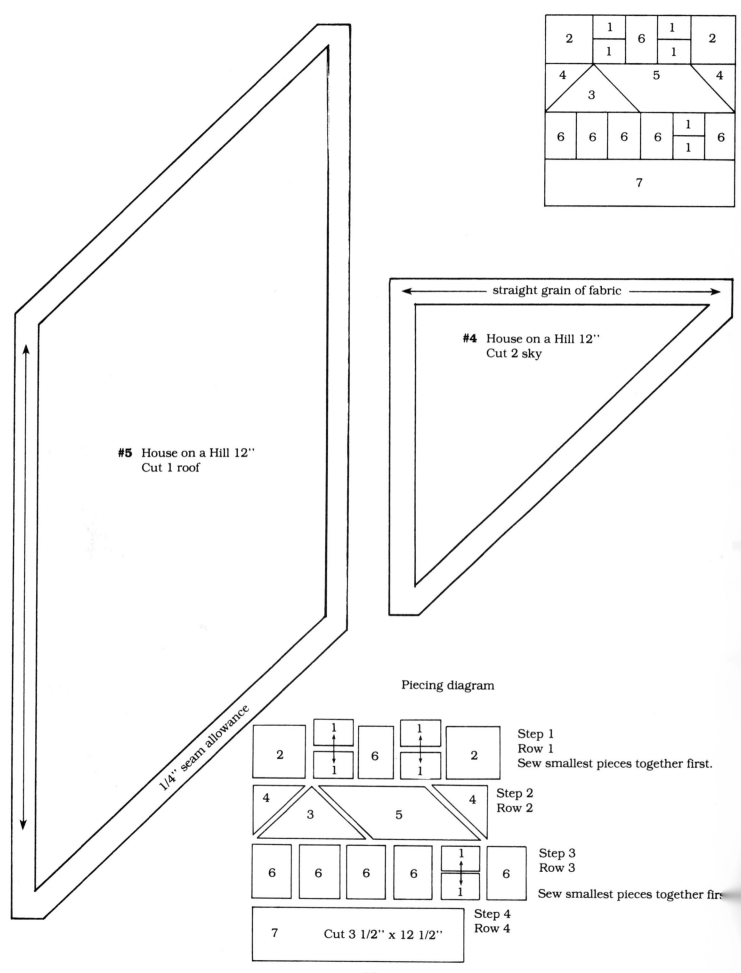

#5 House on a Hill 12"
Cut 1 roof

1/4" seam allowance

straight grain of fabric

#4 House on a Hill 12"
Cut 2 sky

Piecing diagram

Step 1
Row 1
Sew smallest pieces together first.

Step 2
Row 2

Step 3
Row 3

Sew smallest pieces together firs[

Step 4
Row 4

7   Cut 3 1/2" x 12 1/2"

16

Schoolhouse

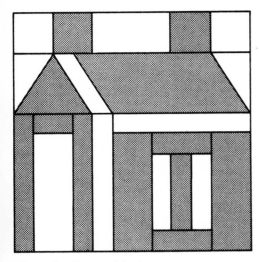

12" Schoolhouse block

Schoolhouse Quilt 65" x 80"

Color:

Turkey red combines with muslin to create a strong graphic quilt complete with Sawtooth[5] border, as shown in the quilt on page 47. You can vary this design by using a different red print for each House block.

Dimensions: 65" x 80"

Measurements for borders and pattern pieces include 1/4" seam allowances.

Materials: 45"-wide fabric

3 1/2 yds. red fabric for houses, outside border and bias binding
2 5/8 yds. muslin for background, lattice and inside border
3 3/4 yds. fabric for backing
72" x 90" Mountain Mist® batting

Directions:

This quilt has an inside muslin border, a pieced Sawtooth border and an outside border with straight sewn corners. For outside border, cut from red fabric two 6" x 69 1/2" strips for length and two 6" x 65 1/2" strips for width. For inside border, cut from muslin two 3 1/2" x 63 1/2" strips for length and two 3 1/2" x 42" strips for width.

2. From muslin, cut three 3 1/2" x 42 1/2" lattice strips and eight 3 1/2" x 12 1/2" lattice strips.
3. Cut and piece 12 Schoolhouse blocks.
4. Set three pieced Schoolhouse blocks together with 3 1/2" x 12 1/2" lattice strips. Join four rows of blocks and lattice strips together for quilt top.
5. Add straight sewn muslin border.
6. Make Sawtooth border. Using pattern piece #12, cut 74 red triangles and 74 muslin triangles. Sew the muslin and red fabric triangles together to make 74 squares. Cut four 3 1/2" muslin squares.
7. Join 21 Sawtooth segments to each side of quilt, making sure triangle seams line up with lattice and quilt block seams. Join 16 Sawtooth segments to top and bottom of quilt, adding a plain muslin block at each corner.
8. Add straight sewn red borders.
9. Add batting and backing, then quilt or tie. Quilting suggestion: Quilt two rows of horizontal lines through the quilt blocks, creating the illusion of "logs." Quilt 1/4" inside each triangle in the Sawtooth border. The wide border will allow effective use of a cable or fan pattern.
10. Bind with bias strips of red fabric.

5. *The Sawtooth border reminded early quilters of the saws used to clear their land.*

17

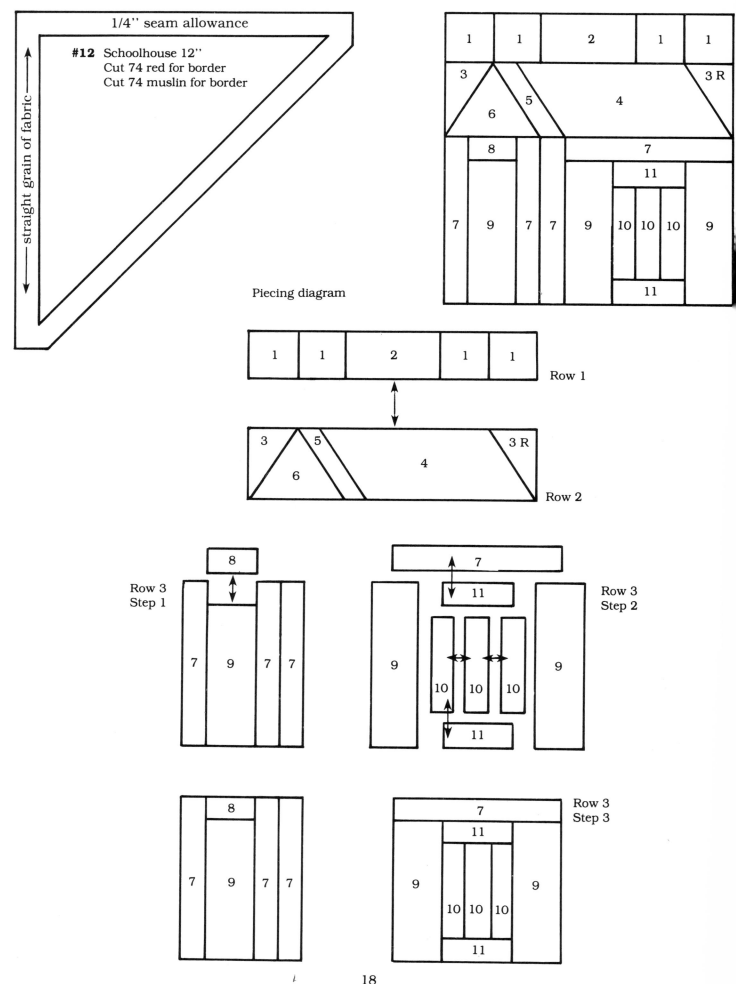

1/4" seam allowance

#12 Schoolhouse 12"
Cut 74 red for border
Cut 74 muslin for border

straight grain of fabric

Piecing diagram

| 1 | 1 | 2 | 1 | 1 | Row 1

| 3 | 5 | 4 | 3 R | 6 | Row 2

Row 3
Step 1

Row 3
Step 2

Row 3
Step 3

18

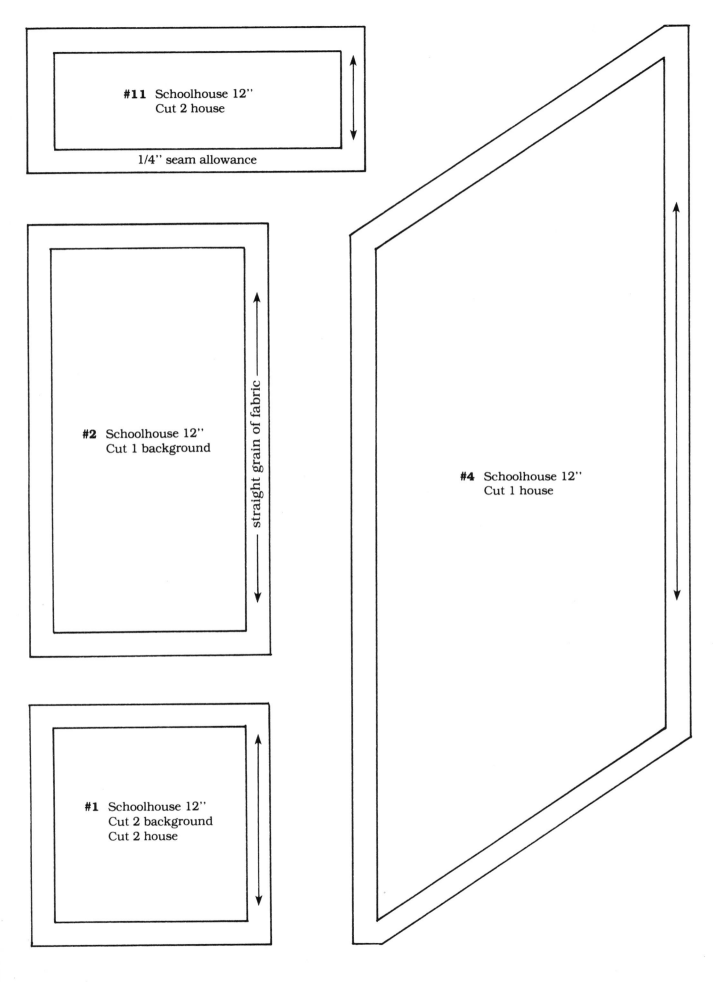

#11 Schoolhouse 12"
Cut 2 house

1/4" seam allowance

#2 Schoolhouse 12"
Cut 1 background

straight grain of fabric

#4 Schoolhouse 12"
Cut 1 house

#1 Schoolhouse 12"
Cut 2 background
Cut 2 house

19

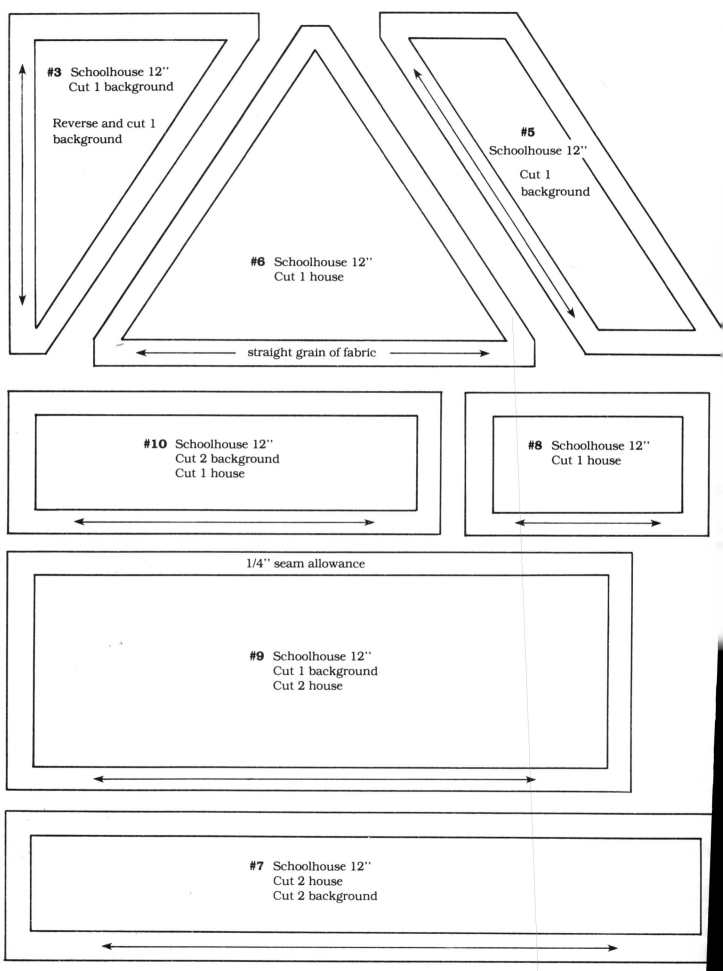

#3 Schoolhouse 12"
Cut 1 background

Reverse and cut 1
background

#5
Schoolhouse 12"

Cut 1
background

#6 Schoolhouse 12"
Cut 1 house

straight grain of fabric

#10 Schoolhouse 12"
Cut 2 background
Cut 1 house

#8 Schoolhouse 12"
Cut 1 house

1/4" seam allowance

#9 Schoolhouse 12"
Cut 1 background
Cut 2 house

#7 Schoolhouse 12"
Cut 2 house
Cut 2 background

House Quilt® 6

12" House block

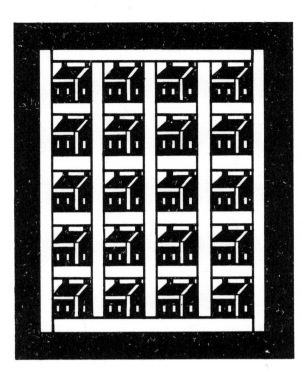

House Quilt 74" x 89"

Color:

Combine a dark print or solid with plain muslin to achieve crisp contrast. This quilt is shown in Plate 4 on page 42.

Dimensions: 74" x 89"

Measurements for borders and pattern pieces include 1/4" seam allowances.

Materials: 45"-wide fabric
3 1/2 yds. dark print or solid for houses and borders
3 yds. muslin for background and lattice
5 1/2 yds. fabric for backing
81" x 96" Mountain Mist® batting

©*Pamela Reising for Stearns & Foster.*

Directions:

1. This quilt has simple borders with straight sewn corners. From muslin, cut two 3 1/2" x 57 1/2" strips for width and two 3 1/2" x 78 1/2" strips for length. For second border, cut two 5 3/4" x 63" strips for width and two 5 3/4" x 89" strips for length from dark print.
2. Cut 16 lattice strips 3 1/2" x 12 1/2" and three lattice strips 3 1/2" x 72 1/2".
3. Cut and piece 20 House blocks.
4. Set five pieced House blocks together with short lattice strips to make columns. Join four columns of blocks and lattice strips together for quilt top.
5. Add straight sewn borders.
6. Add batting and backing, then quilt or tie. Quilting suggestion: Quilt 1/4" from all seamlines on House blocks, lattices and borders.
7. Bind with bias strips of either muslin or dark fabric.

Piecing diagram

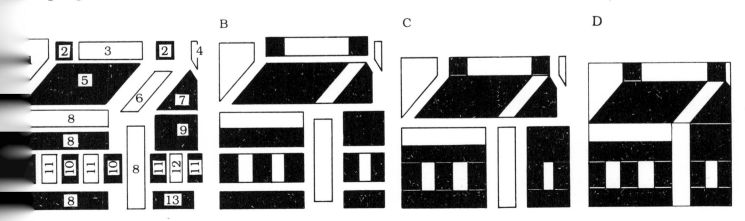

21

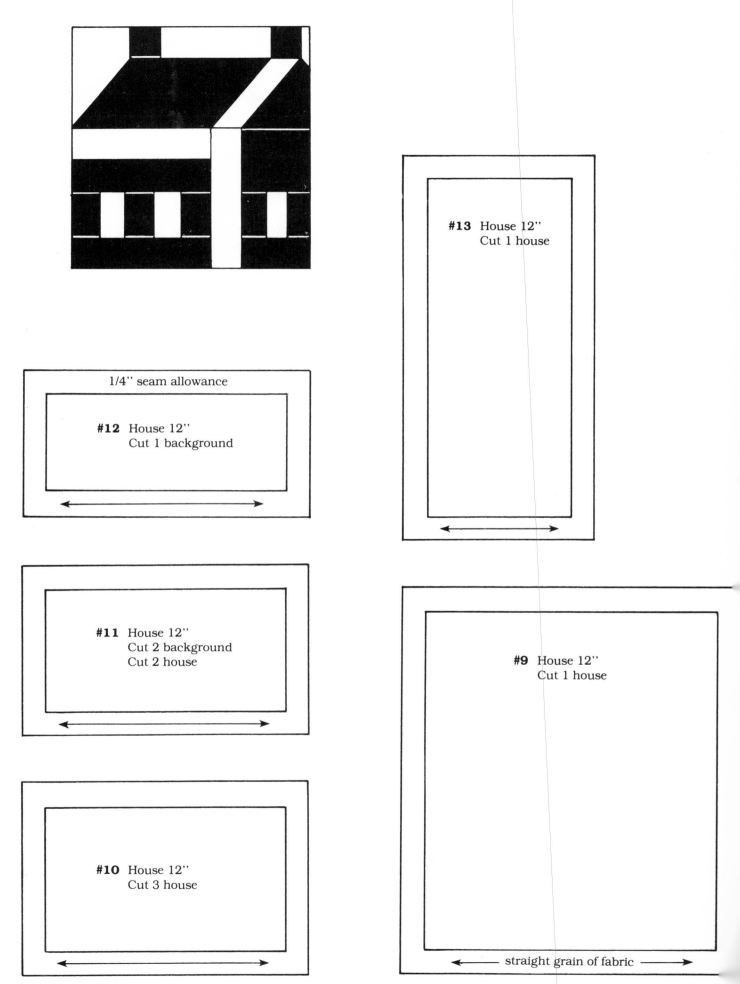

1/4" seam allowance

#12 House 12"
Cut 1 background

#11 House 12"
Cut 2 background
Cut 2 house

#10 House 12"
Cut 3 house

#13 House 12"
Cut 1 house

#9 House 12"
Cut 1 house

straight grain of fabric

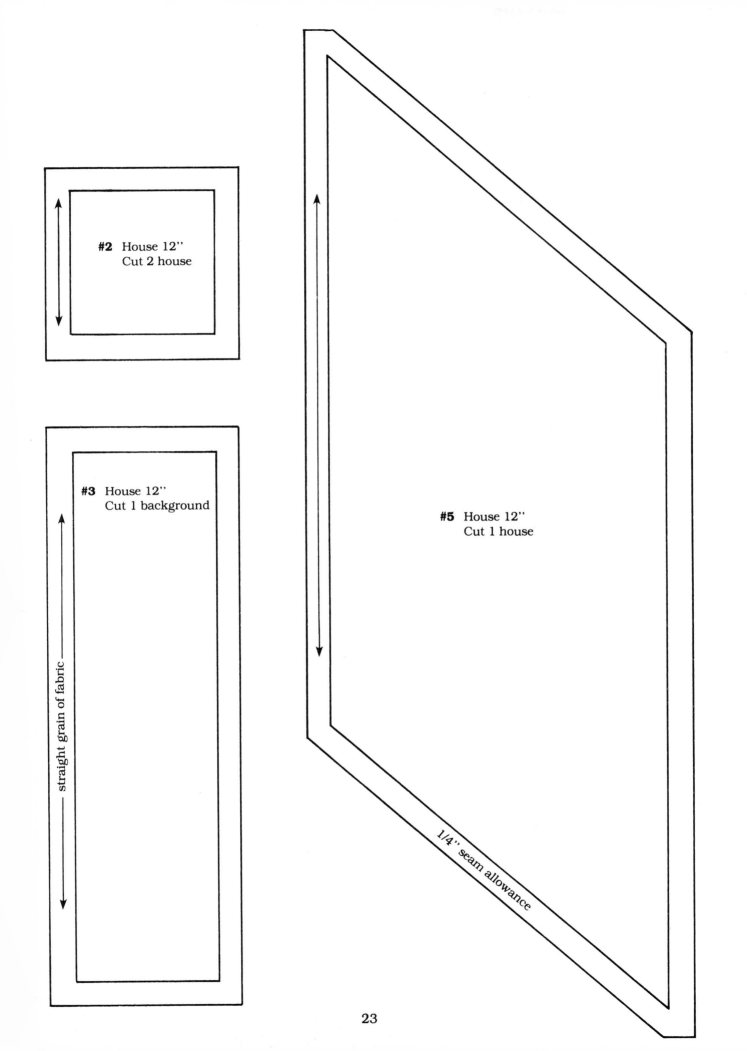

#2 House 12''
Cut 2 house

#3 House 12''
Cut 1 background

straight grain of fabric

#5 House 12''
Cut 1 house

1/4'' seam allowance

23

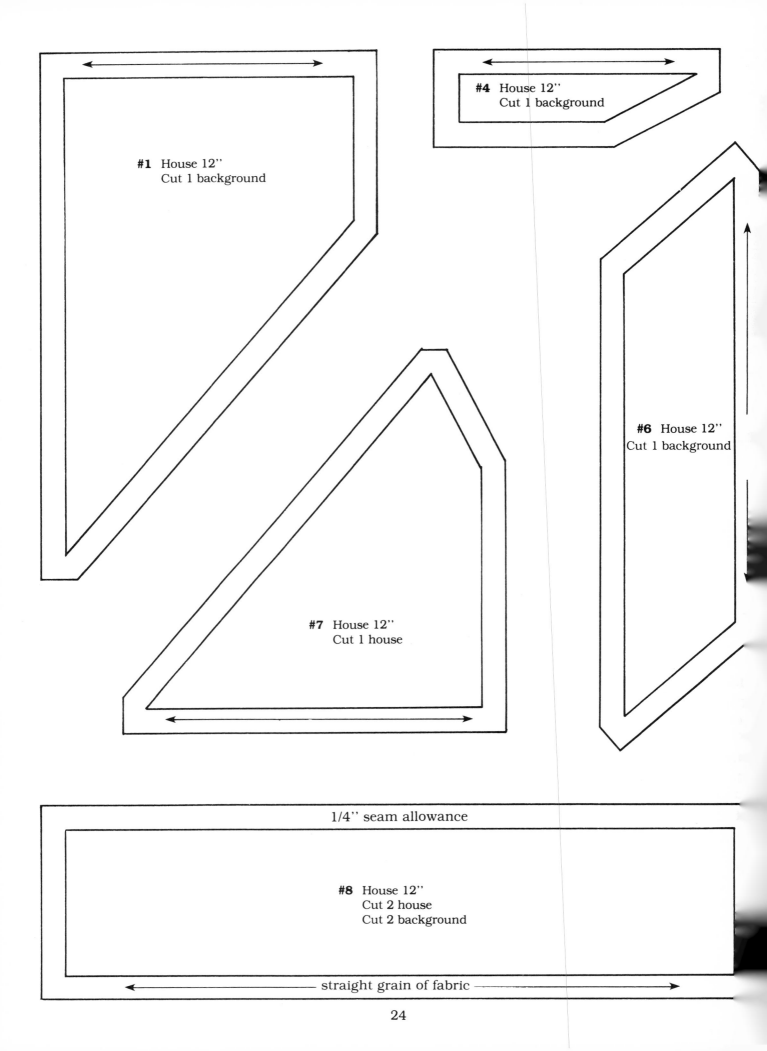

#1 House 12"
Cut 1 background

#4 House 12"
Cut 1 background

#6 House 12"
Cut 1 background

#7 House 12"
Cut 1 house

1/4" seam allowance

#8 House 12"
Cut 2 house
Cut 2 background

straight grain of fabric

24

omforts of Home Quilt©⁷

House block

Sawtooth Star Block

or:

his giant Nine Patch features a green House ck surrounded by red Sawtooth Star blocks, unred muslin blocks, and a red Sawtooth border.

iensions: 48" x 48"

easurements for borders and pattern pieces inle 1/4" seam allowances.

terials: 45"-wide fabric

yds. muslin for background and alternating
blocks
4 yd. green fabric for House block
1/4 yds. red fabric for Sawtooth Star blocks, Sawtooth border and binding
yds. fabric for backing
ountain Mist® batting, crib size

Comforts of Home Quilt 48" x 48"

Directions:

1. This quilt has a pieced Sawtooth border and an outer border with straight sewn corners. From muslin, cut two 3 1/2" x 48 1/2" strips and two 3 1/2" x 42 1/2" strips.
2. Cut and piece one House block. Refer to pages 21-24 for templates and piecing diagram.
3. Cut and piece four Sawtooth Star blocks.
4. Cut four 12 1/2" x 12 1/2" square blocks from muslin.
5. Set together House block, Sawtooth Star blocks and muslin blocks, using the diagram as a guide to placement.
6. Cut 52 triangles from both muslin and red fabric and piece Sawtooth border, using the diagram as a guide to placement.
7. Add straight sewn muslin borders.
8. Add batting and backing, then quilt or tie. Quilting suggestion: Quilt 1/4" away from each seam. Feathered circles can be quilted in the 12" blocks and Sawtooth Star centers.
9. Bind with bias strips of red fabric.

7. ©*Pamela Reising*

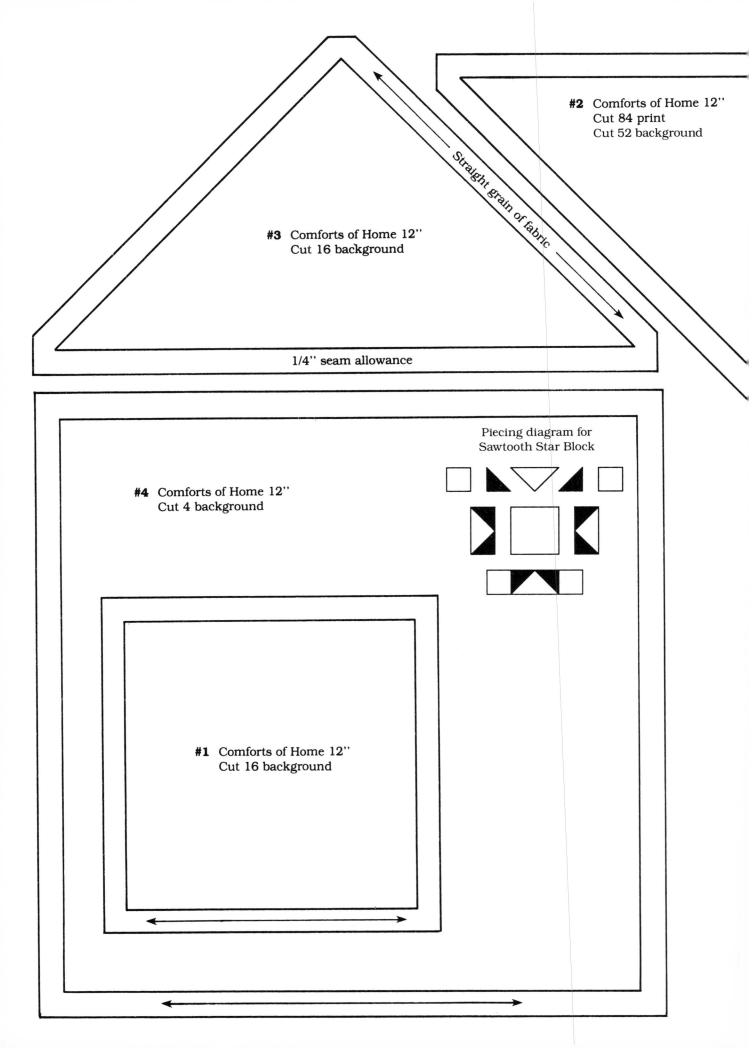

#2 Comforts of Home 12"
Cut 84 print
Cut 52 background

Straight grain of fabric

#3 Comforts of Home 12"
Cut 16 background

1/4" seam allowance

Piecing diagram for
Sawtooth Star Block

#4 Comforts of Home 12"
Cut 4 background

#1 Comforts of Home 12"
Cut 16 background

House

'' House block

House Quilt 68" x 80"

olor:

Dark blue House blocks with red chimneys express a strong design statement, echoed by the ieced border. The robust effect is softened by the uilting design in the unpieced blocks.

imensions: 68" x 80"

Measurements for borders and pattern pieces inude 1/4" seam allowances.

Materials: 45"-wide fabric

2 yds. dark blue fabric for houses and border
3 1/2 yds. muslin for background and border
1/2 yd. red fabric for chimneys and binding
4 1/4 yds. fabric for backing
72" x 90" Mountain Mist® batting

ecing diagram

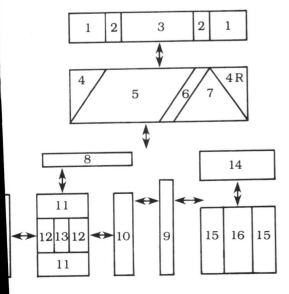

Directions:

1. Cut and piece 15 House blocks.
2. Cut fifteen 12 1/2" x 12 1/2" square blocks from muslin.
3. Set together House and unpieced blocks, using the diagram as a guide to placement.
4. Cut 105 pieces for border from both muslin and dark background fabric. Piece together 70 border segments (35 of each color sequence).

5. Piece together 15 border segments, alternating the color sequence, and attach to top of quilt.
6. Piece together 19 border segments, continuing to alternate color sequence, and piece to right side of quilt.
7. Piece together 16 border segments, continuing to alternate color sequence, and piece to bottom of quilt.
8. Piece together 20 border segments, continuing to alternate color sequence, and piece to left side of quilt.
9. Add batting and backing, then quilt or tie. Quilting suggestion: Quilt 1/4" from all seamlines on House blocks and border. Use the unpieced muslin blocks to display a favorite quilting design such as the feathered circle or spider web design.
10. Bind with bias strips of red fabric.

27

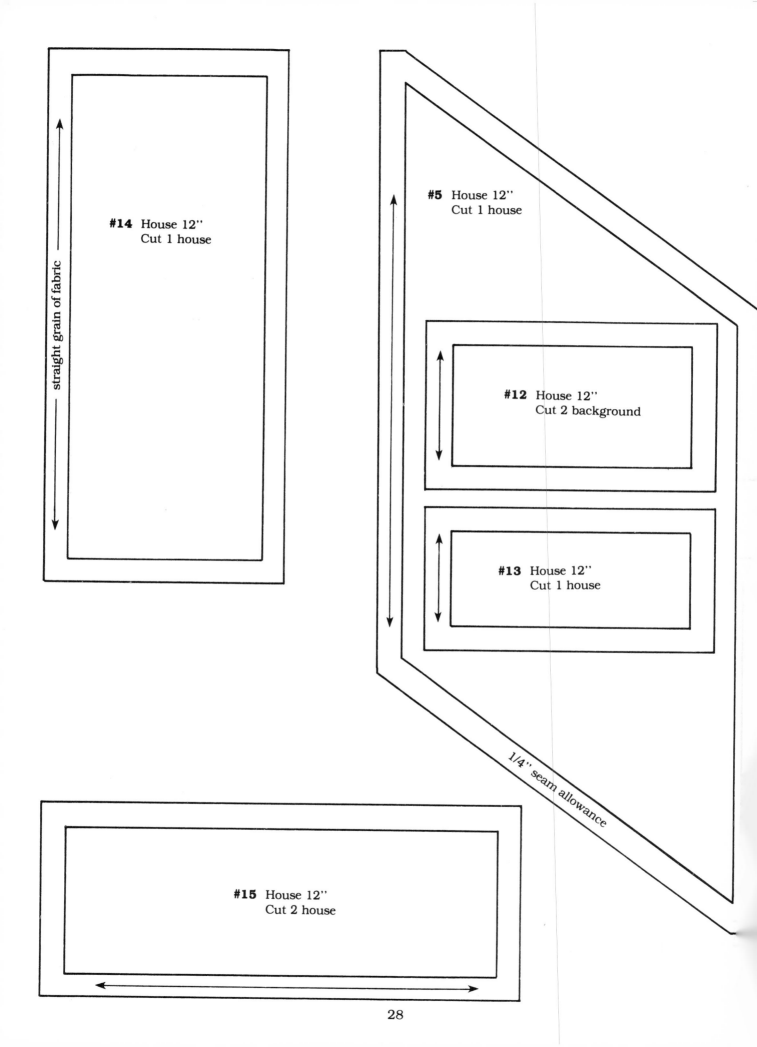

#14 House 12"
Cut 1 house

straight grain of fabric

#5 House 12"
Cut 1 house

#12 House 12"
Cut 2 background

#13 House 12"
Cut 1 house

1/4" seam allowance

#15 House 12"
Cut 2 house

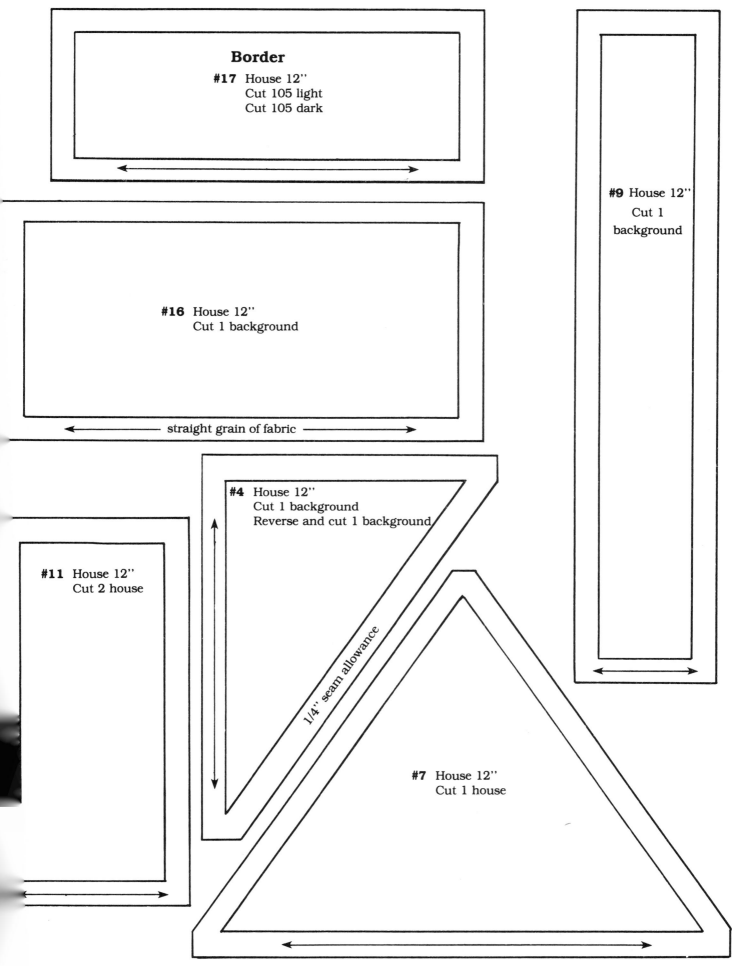

Border

#17 House 12"
Cut 105 light
Cut 105 dark

#9 House 12"
Cut 1
background

#16 House 12"
Cut 1 background

straight grain of fabric

#4 House 12"
Cut 1 background
Reverse and cut 1 background

#11 House 12"
Cut 2 house

1/4" seam allowance

#7 House 12"
Cut 1 house

29

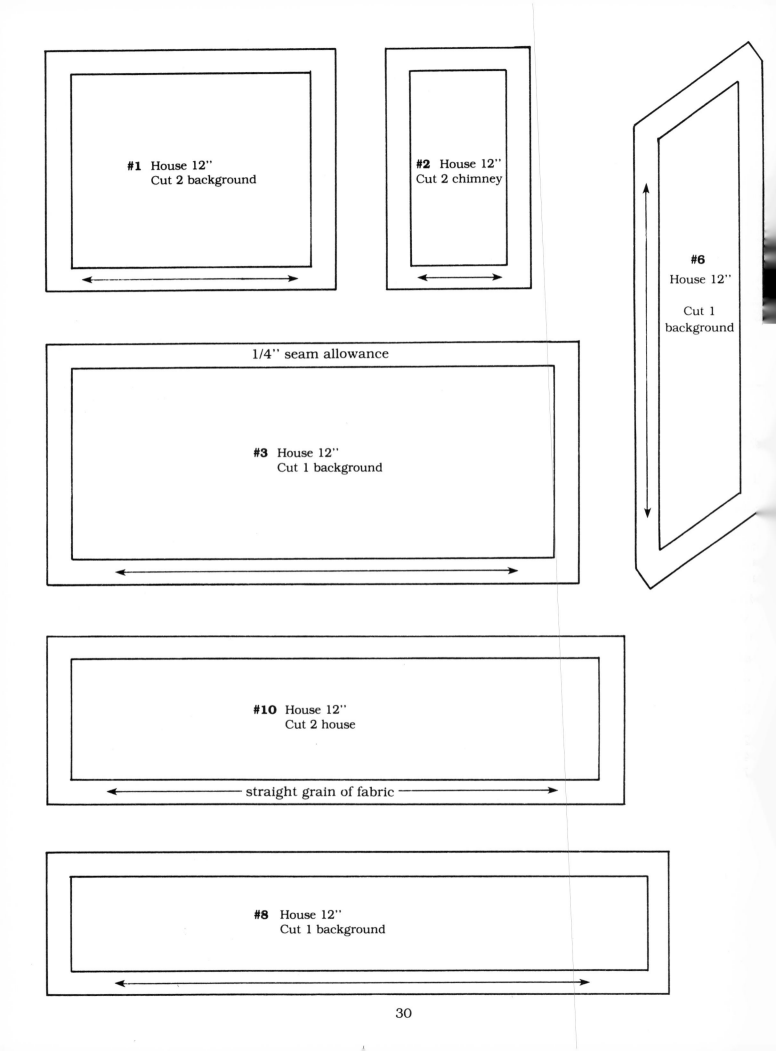

#1 House 12"
Cut 2 background

#2 House 12"
Cut 2 chimney

#6
House 12"

Cut 1
background

1/4" seam allowance

#3 House 12"
Cut 1 background

#10 House 12"
Cut 2 house

straight grain of fabric

#8 House 12"
Cut 1 background

Schoolhouse

1" Schoolhouse block

I   II   III

Alternate Blocks

Color:

Red Schoolhouses on a muslin background are combined with pieced triangle blocks to form a Barn-raising set. The wide green borders anchor this geometric design.

Dimensions: 67" x 89"

Measurements for borders and pattern pieces include 1/4" seam allowances.

Materials: 45"-wide fabric

2 1/2 yds. red fabric for Schoolhouses and binding
3 yds. muslin for background, triangles and border corners
2 1/4 yds. green fabric for triangles and border
4 yds. fabric for backing
72" x 90" Mountain Mist® batting

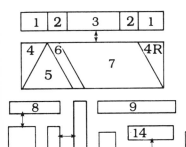

Piecing diagram

Schoolhouse Quilt 67" x 89"

Directions:

1. This quilt has simple borders with straight sewn corners and corner blocks. From green fabric, cut two 6 1/2" x 77 1/2" strips and two 6 1/2" x 55 1/2" strips. From muslin, cut four 6 1/2" square corner blocks.
2. Cut and piece 18 Schoolhouse blocks.
3. Cut 12 triangles, using Set Piece A, from both muslin and green fabric. Piece together to make 12 Alternate Blocks I.
4. Cut two triangles, using Set Piece B, from both muslin and green fabric. Piece together to make Alternate Block II.
5. Cut four triangles from green, using Set Piece B. Cut 12 triangles from muslin, using Set Piece B. Piece together to make four Alternate Blocks III.
6. Set Schoolhouse blocks and alternate blocks together, using the diagram above as a guide to placement. Note that the geometric effect of this quilt is emphasized by setting the Schoolhouse blocks in different directions.
7. Add straight sewn borders to top and bottom of quilt.
8. Piece corner blocks on either end of the remaining border strips. Sew border strips to quilt.
9. Add batting and backing, then quilt or tie. Quilting suggestion: Quilt 1/4" from all seamlines on House blocks. Quilt a grid of hanging diamonds through all of the alternate blocks and corner blocks. A cable design can be quilted on the wide borders.
10. Bind with bias strips of red fabric.

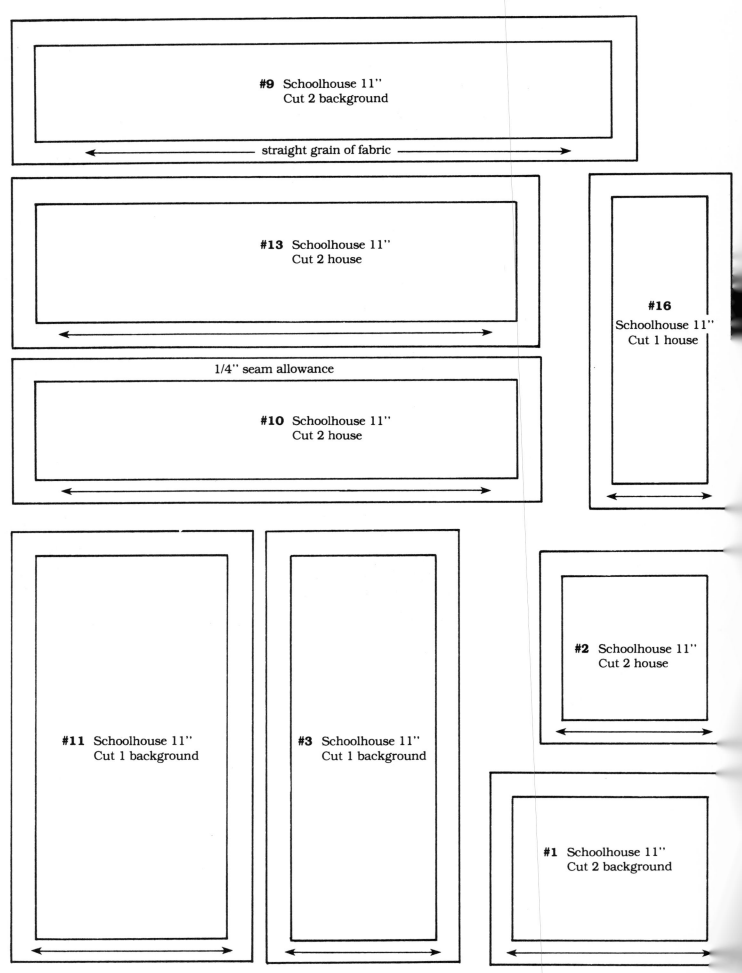

#9 Schoolhouse 11"
Cut 2 background

straight grain of fabric

#13 Schoolhouse 11"
Cut 2 house

#16
Schoolhouse 11"
Cut 1 house

1/4" seam allowance

#10 Schoolhouse 11"
Cut 2 house

#11 Schoolhouse 11"
Cut 1 background

#3 Schoolhouse 11"
Cut 1 background

#2 Schoolhouse 11"
Cut 2 house

#1 Schoolhouse 11"
Cut 2 background

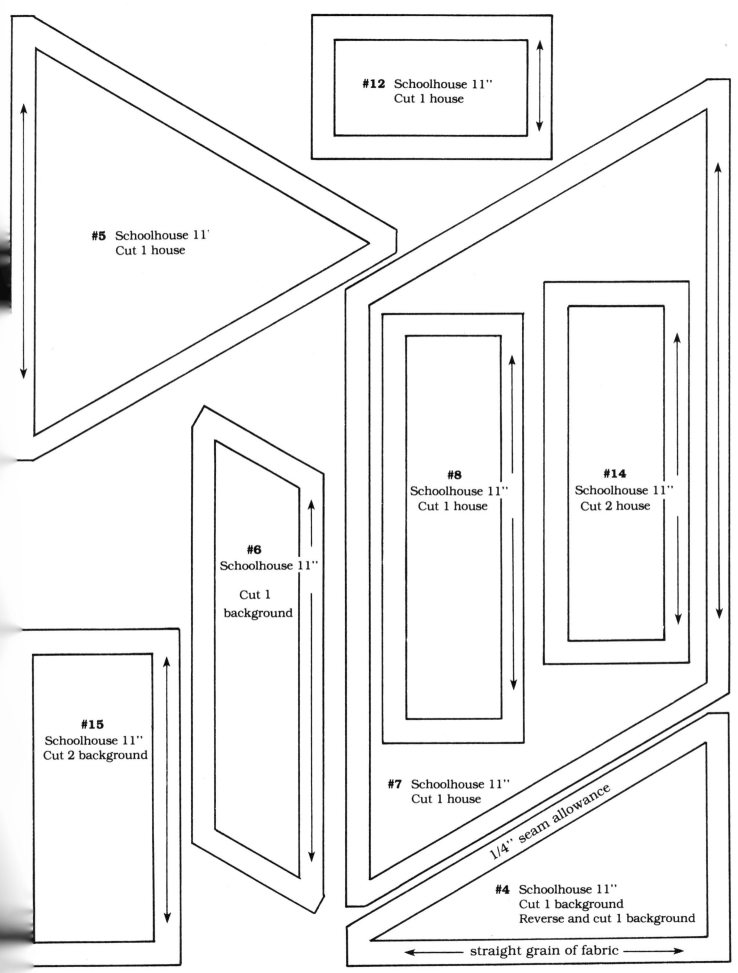

#12 Schoolhouse 11"
Cut 1 house

#5 Schoolhouse 11"
Cut 1 house

#8
Schoolhouse 11"
Cut 1 house

#14
Schoolhouse 11"
Cut 2 house

#6
Schoolhouse 11"

Cut 1
background

#15
Schoolhouse 11"
Cut 2 background

#7 Schoolhouse 11"
Cut 1 house

1/4" seam allowance

#4 Schoolhouse 11"
Cut 1 background
Reverse and cut 1 background

← straight grain of fabric →

33

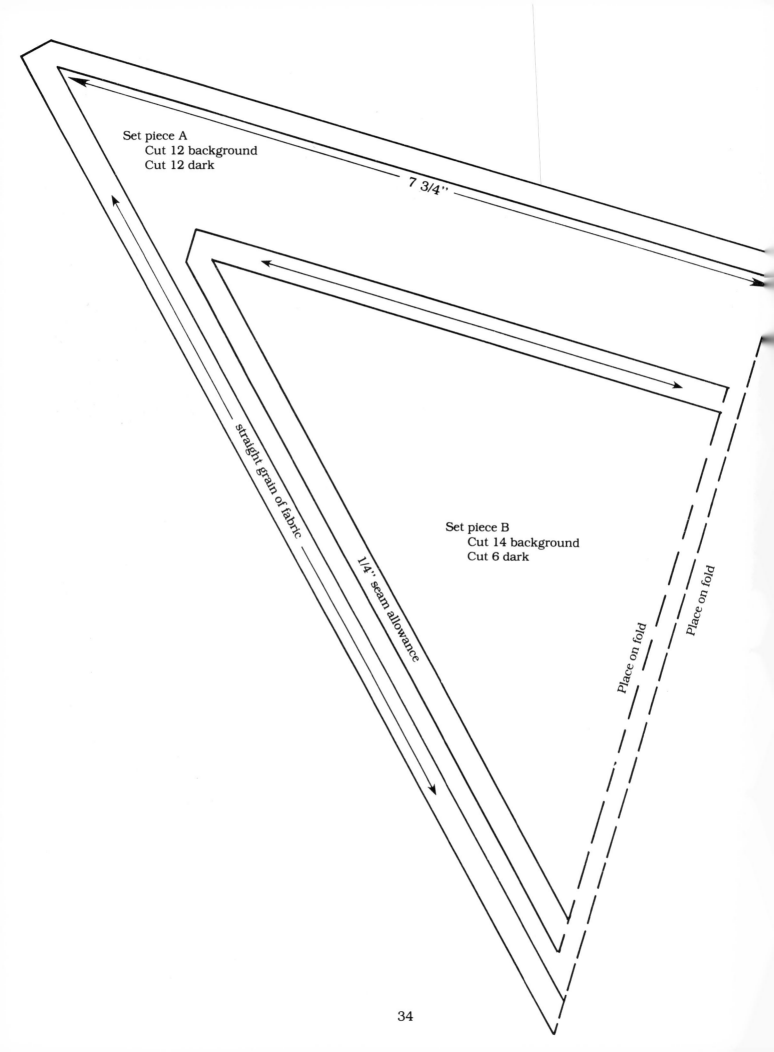

Set piece A
   Cut 12 background
   Cut 12 dark

7 3/4"

straight grain of fabric

1/4" seam allowance

Set piece B
   Cut 14 background
   Cut 6 dark

Place on fold

Place on fold

34

Cabin Raising

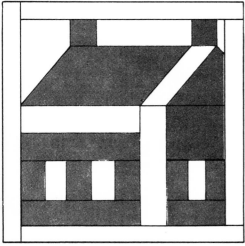

10" House block

0" Log Cabin block

Cabin Raising Quilt 70" x 70"

olor:

Each Log Cabin block is made from dark and light ackground fabrics. Choose one of the dark and one the light background fabrics for the House block. he blocks are set together using the Barnraising sign, hence the name "Cabin Raising." This quilt shown in Plate 2 on page 42.

mensions: 70" x 70"

Measurements for borders and pattern pieces in- de 1/4" seam allowances.

terials: 45"-wide fabric

    /4 yd. solid color fabric for center squares
    2 yds. dark fabric for border and bias binding
    /2 yd. light background fabric A
    /2 yd. light background fabric B
    /2 yd. light background fabric C
    1/8 yds. light background fabric D
    yd. dark background fabric E
    yd. dark background fabric F
    yd. dark background fabric G
    1/4 yds. dark background fabric H

4 yds. fabric for backing
72" x 90" Mountain Mist® batting

Directions:

1. This quilt has a simple border with straight sewn corners. From dark fabric, cut two 5 1/4" x 60 1/2" strips for width and two 5 1/4" x 70" strips for length.
2. Cut and piece eight House blocks, using fabric D for background and fabric H for house. Refer to pages 21-22 for piecing diagram. Sew a #14 strip to right edge, a #15 strip to top and bottom and a #16 strip to left edge of each block.
3. Cut and piece 28 Log Cabin blocks, using the dark and light background fabrics in varying positions in each block. Use each fabric twice in each block. Several templates are used for both the House and Log Cabin blocks.
4. Set pieced blocks together, using the diagram above as a guide to placement of House and Log Cabin blocks. Note the position of the dark and light sides of the Log Cabin blocks. Arrange blocks so that the outer strips are of different fabrics.
5. Add straight sewn borders.
6. Add batting and backing, then quilt or tie. Quilting suggestion: Quilt 1/4" inside each solid Log Cabin center square. Quilt down the middle of each Log Cabin strip, working from the center to the edges in one continuous spiral. Quilt in the middle of each House section.
7. Bind with bias strips of border fabric.

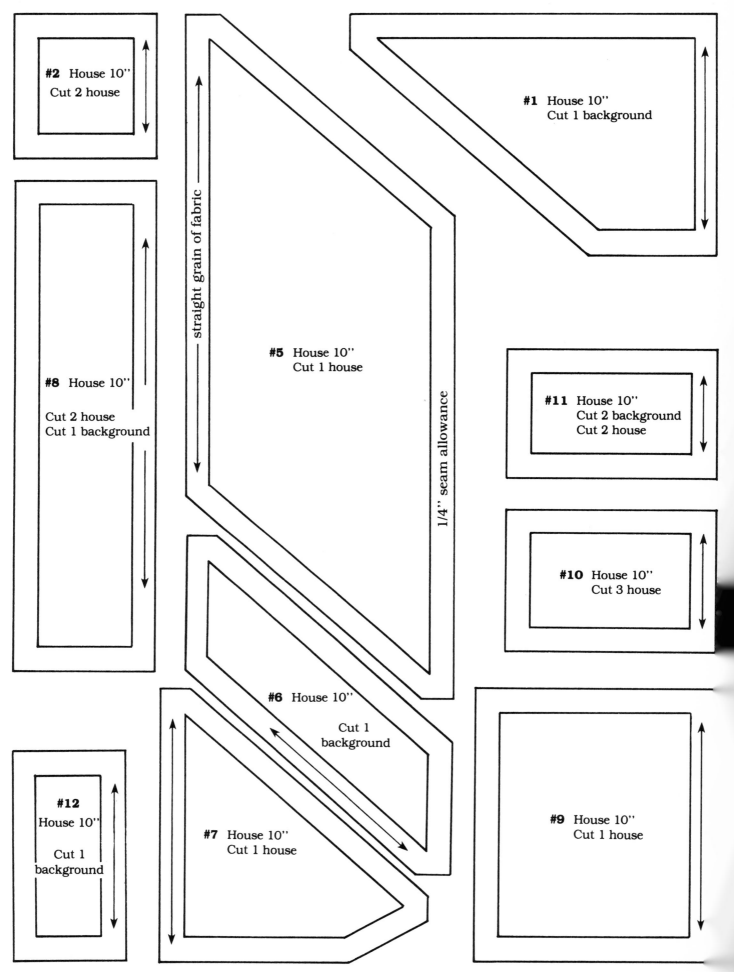

#2 House 10"
Cut 2 house

#1 House 10"
Cut 1 background

straight grain of fabric

#5 House 10"
Cut 1 house

#8 House 10"

Cut 2 house
Cut 1 background

1/4" seam allowance

#11 House 10"
Cut 2 background
Cut 2 house

#10 House 10"
Cut 3 house

#6 House 10"

Cut 1
background

#12
House 10"

Cut 1
background

#7 House 10"
Cut 1 house

#9 House 10"
Cut 1 house

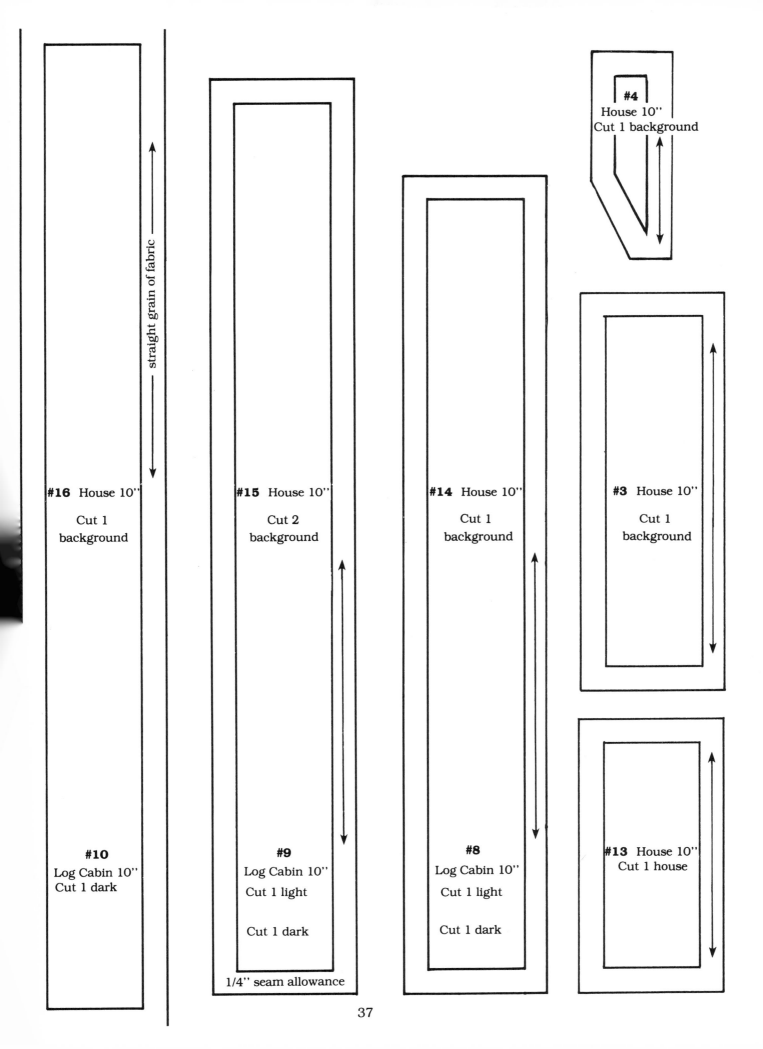

straight grain of fabric

#16 House 10"

Cut 1
background

#10
Log Cabin 10"
Cut 1 dark

#15 House 10"

Cut 2
background

#9
Log Cabin 10"

Cut 1 light

Cut 1 dark

1/4" seam allowance

#14 House 10"

Cut 1
background

#8
Log Cabin 10"

Cut 1 light

Cut 1 dark

#4
House 10"
Cut 1 background

#3 House 10"

Cut 1
background

#13 House 10"
Cut 1 house

37

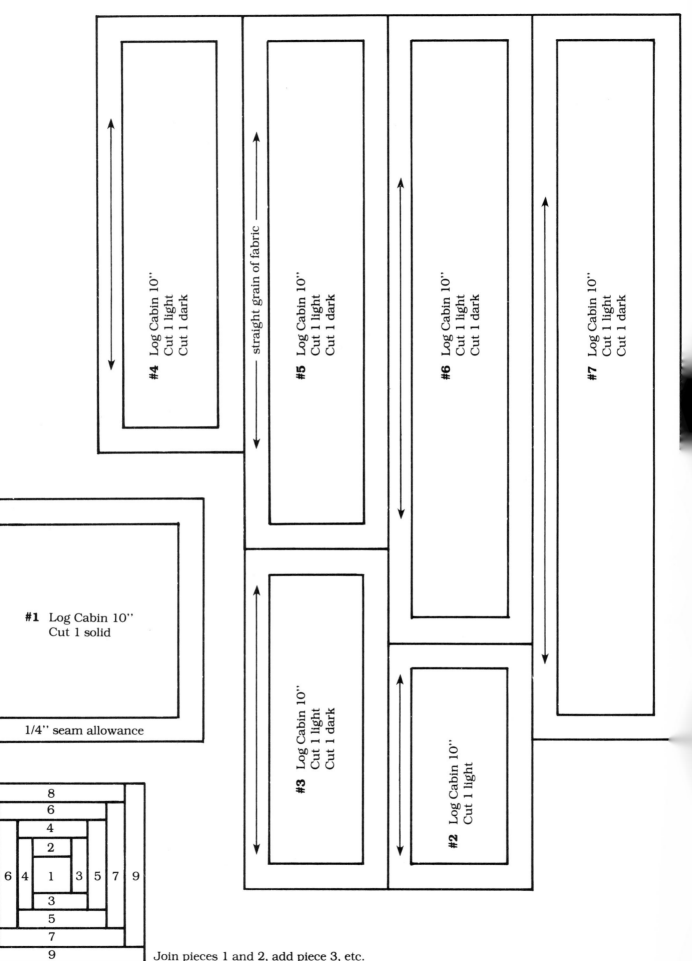

#4 Log Cabin 10"
Cut 1 light
Cut 1 dark

straight grain of fabric

#5 Log Cabin 10"
Cut 1 light
Cut 1 dark

#6 Log Cabin 10"
Cut 1 light
Cut 1 dark

#7 Log Cabin 10"
Cut 1 light
Cut 1 dark

#1 Log Cabin 10"
Cut 1 solid

1/4" seam allowance

#3 Log Cabin 10"
Cut 1 light
Cut 1 dark

#2 Log Cabin 10"
Cut 1 light

| | | 8 | | |
| 6 |
| 4 |
| 2 |
| 10 | 8 | 6 | 4 | 1 | 3 | 5 | 7 | 9 |
| 3 |
| 5 |
| 7 |
| 9 |

Join pieces 1 and 2, add piece 3, etc.

38

School House Quilt©8

8'' School House block

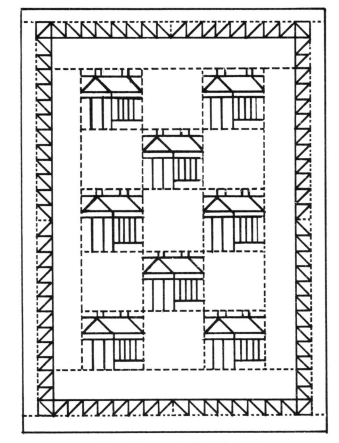

School House Quilt 40'' x 56''

Color:

Eight different prints were used to make this delightful quilt. The fabrics used for the School Houses are repeated in order in the Sawtooth border. Make this a scrapbag project, as shown in Plate 12 on page 45, or choose only one print for the School Houses and pieced border.

Dimensions: 40'' x 56''

Measurements for borders and pattern pieces include 1/4'' seam allowances.

Materials: 45''-wide fabric

2 yds. muslin or small print for background
1/4 yd. each of eight different prints for School Houses and Sawtooth border (or 1 1/2 yds. of one print or equivalent scraps)
1 5/8 yds. fabric for backing
1/2 yd. print fabric for binding
Mountain Mist® batting, crib size

Directions:

Cut borders from muslin background fabric: For outside border, cut two 2 1/2'' x 52 1/2'' strips for length and two 2 1/2'' x 40 1/2'' strips for width. For inside border, cut two 4 1/2'' x 40 1/2'' strips for length and two 4 1/2'' x 32 1/2'' strips for width.
Cut eight 8 1/2'' x 8 1/2'' square blocks from background fabric.

3. Cut and piece eight School House blocks. Use one fabric for all or make each House from a different print, as shown in Plate 13 on page 41.
4. Sew the eight pieced blocks and the seven background fabric squares together, using the diagram for a guide to placement.
5. For the inside border, add the two 4 1/2'' x 40 1/2'' strips, then the two 4 1/2'' x 32 1/2'' strips.
6. Make Sawtooth border. Using pattern piece #9, cut 84 print triangles and 84 background triangles. Sew the print and background triangles together to make 84 squares. Sew the squares together in strips, as pictured, and add to quilt center.
7. Add the outside border strips with straight sewn corners, sewing the two 2 1/2'' x 52 1/2'' strips for the length first. Add the two 2 1/2'' x 40 1/2'' strips for the width.
8. Add batting and backing, then quilt or tie. Quilting suggestion: Outline quilt Sawtooth border and each School House 1/4'' away from seams. Quilt a diagonal grid as a filler on the muslin, ending at the Sawtooth border. Grid may also be used on the outer border. Quilt inside triangles of Sawtooth border.

8. ©*Marsha McCloskey, 1983*

39

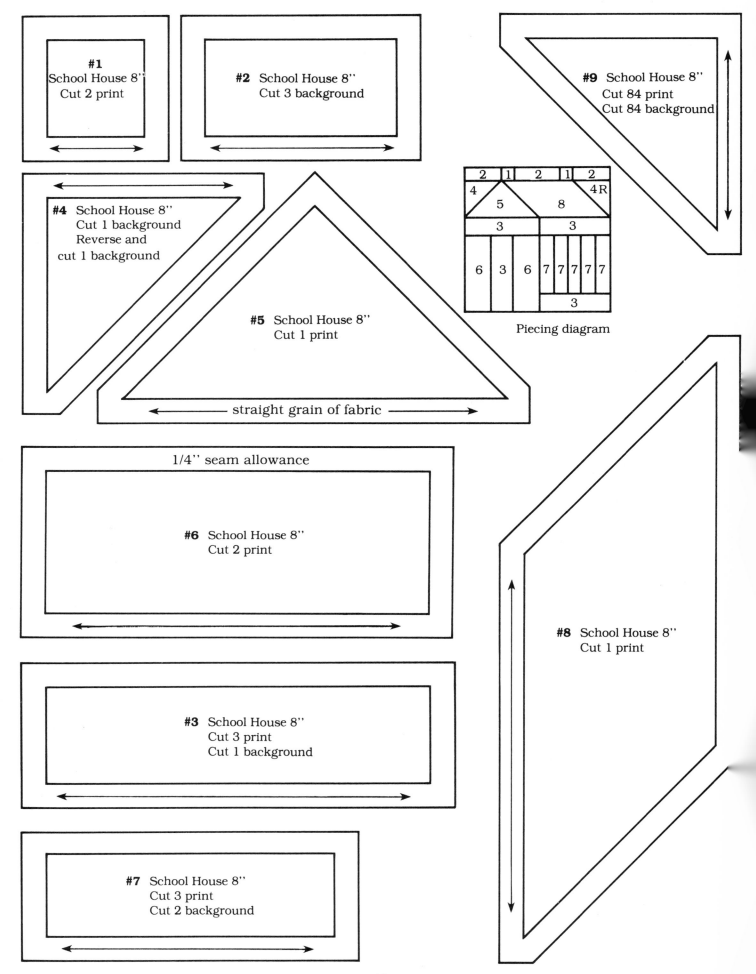

#1
School House 8''
Cut 2 print

#2 School House 8''
Cut 3 background

#9 School House 8''
Cut 84 print
Cut 84 background

#4 School House 8''
Cut 1 background
Reverse and
cut 1 background

#5 School House 8''
Cut 1 print

2	1	2	1	2
4	5		8	4R
3			3	
6	3	6	7 7 7 7 7	
			3	

Piecing diagram

straight grain of fabric

1/4'' seam allowance

#6 School House 8''
Cut 2 print

#8 School House 8''
Cut 1 print

#3 School House 8''
Cut 3 print
Cut 1 background

#7 School House 8''
Cut 3 print
Cut 2 background

40

Plate 1

Plate 1: A House on a Hill Quilt, done in muted fabrics, sets the color scheme in this country kitchen. Hand painted plates featuring house motifs and matching placemats decorate the table. The motif is repeated on a house sampler and kitchen towel.

41

Plate 2: Log Cabin and House blocks make use of light and dark contrasts in this barnraising set. 72" x 72". Quilted by Freda Smith.

Plate 3: House on a Hill by Nicki Plath uses wide muslin lattice and borders around each house in this "scrap" quilt. 86" x 102". Each house is embellished with laces, trims and embroidery, then framed with colorful fabric strips.

Plate 4: House Quilt, by Pamela J. Reising for Stearns and Foster, uses a navy print with muslin to create a delightful contrast. 70" x 106". This house pattern has a quaint charm which is enhanced by the repetition of identical blocks.

Plate 2

Plate 3

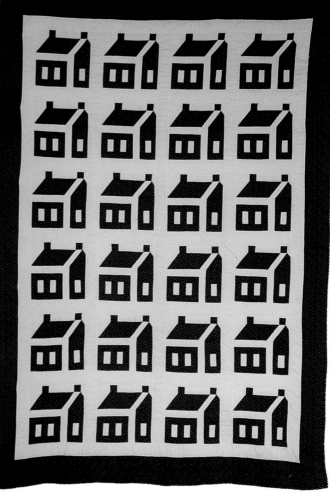

Plate 4

These three strong graphic quilts all use a House or Schoolhouse block set in a different manner.

Plate 5: The Comforts of Home Quilt, designed by Pamela J. Reising, uses Sawtooth Stars and a Sawtooth border around a House block. 48" x 48". Feathered wreaths quilted into the alternate blocks add a nice contrast to the angular lines.

Plate 6: Pieced quilt, House, 82" x 72", uses an alternating block set with an interesting pieced border. This quilt was made in Ohio between 1900 and 1920. (America Hurrah Antiques, N.Y.C.).

Plate 7: Pieced quilt, Schoolhouse, 1930-1940, New York State. 89" x 66". This fascinating geometric arrangement of the Schoolhouse pattern emphasizes the decorative importance of the white strips, doors, and windows of the red motifs. (Kelter-Malce Antiques).

Plate 5

Plate 6

Plate 7

Plate 8

Plate

Plate 8: A House on a Hill block decorates the front of a perky pinafore.

Plate 9: Applique quilt, Home Sweet Home, 1930-1940. 89" x 70". Very probably this bright tribute to hearth and home is made from one of the many fine quilt patterns issued in the 1930s. (Thos. K. Woodard: American Antiques & Quilts).

Plate 10: Little Love Nest features pastel houses framed by lattice. 14¾" x 20". Appliqued hearts and a quilted heart border echo the romantic theme.

44

Plate 10

Plate 11

Plate 12

Plate 13

Plate 11: Cabin in the Country uses a blue background print to suggest swirling snow between the School House and tree blocks. 46"x 46". A tree border effectively frames the quilt. Quilted by Freda Smith.

Plate 12: School House by Marsha McCloskey is a bright colorful creation of School House blocks surrounded by a Sawtooth border. 40" x 56". The red School House block in the upper left corner faces right and represents the schoolhouse; the other blocks facing left are the houses in the town. Many house quilts do represent towns with layouts that resemble maps.

Plate 13: House on a Corner features screen-printed House blocks framed with a double border. 38"×38". Quilting by Freda Smith features a cable design evenly divided between the borders.

Plate 14

Plate 14: *Little Red Schoolhouse: Morning, Noon, and Night was designed by Jane M. Patterson and Dott Stone for the Little Red Schoolhouse Quilt Guild, and the members did the quilting. Jane observed: "Starting with the earliest light, as Teacher would have seen it when she came to get the day started, the colors move down through the busy, bright, boisterous school day to the jewel-glow of lamp-lighted windows at night."*

Plate 15

Plate 15: *Schoolhouse Quilt has a primitive "folk-art" look created by using "turkey red" against muslin. 62" x 76". The quilt is framed with a Sawtooth border of patchwork and an outer border is quilted in a fan design. Two horizontal rows of quilting lines (a design often used by Amish quilters) give the effect of logs on the houses. Quilted by Freda Smith.*

Plate 16: Pieced quilt, School-house, dated 1891, Pennsylvania. 78" x 80". The Schoolhouse pattern is one of the most familiar in American quilts; here it has been magically used to create a whole town, said to be York, Pennsylvania. The moon and stars look down on almost sixty structures, including two churches with graveyards, and buildings labeled "Coal," "Barn," and "Union Depot." The special touch is the railroad complete with telegraph poles. This is an entrancing example of American folk art. (Collection of Linda Pracilio).

Plate

Plate 17

Plate 17: Pillows made from House on a Hill and Little Love Nest blocks effectively combine shades of brown.

Plate 18: Irish Road to Home features stenciled blocks and a quilted vine border. 31" x 31". Quilted by Freda Smith.

Pla

Cabin in the Country

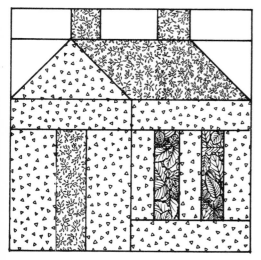

8" School House block

Tree half block   4" corner block

Cabin in the Country 46" x 46"

Color:

Houses in muted colors are surrounded by blue fabric which suggests swirling snow in the background and lattice pieces. The strip pieced trees are forest green and provide nice contrast as a border to frame the grouping of houses and trees.

Dimensions: 46" x 46"

Measurements for borders and pattern pieces include 1/4" seam allowances.

Materials: 45"-wide fabric

1 5/8 yds. blue fabric for background and lattice
3/8 yd. fabric for houses
1/4 yd. fabric for roofs, doors and chimneys
1/8 yd. fabric for windows
1/8 yd. each of five assorted green fabrics for strip pieced trees
1/8 yd. fabric for tree trunks
3 yds. fabric for backing
72" x 90" Mountain Mist® batting

Directions:

1. This quilt has a pieced tree border and an outer border with straight sewn seams. From blue background fabric, cut two 2 1/2" x 42 1/2" strips and two 2 1/2" x 46 1/2" strips.
2. Cut and piece six School House blocks. Refer to page 40 for templates and piecing diagram.
3. Make strip pieced yardage, using 1 1/4"- to 2"-wide strips of green fabric. Cut tree pieces from this yardage.

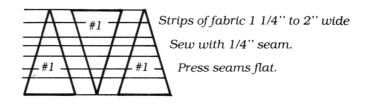

Strips of fabric 1 1/4" to 2" wide

Sew with 1/4" seam.

Press seams flat.

4. Cut and piece six tree half blocks.
5. From blue background fabric, cut 12 lattice strips 3" x 8 1/2". Piece lattice strips, School House blocks and tree half blocks into rows, using the diagram as a guide to placement.
6. Cut four 3" x 34 1/2" lattice strips from blue background fabric. Piece lattice strips and rows of blocks and strips together to form quilt top, referring to diagram for placement.

7. For tree border, make strip pieced yardage, using 1/2"- to 1"-wide strips of green fabric. Cut 68 from strip pieced yardage, using pattern piece 5. Cut 64 pieces from background fabric, using pattern piece 5. Cut 8 pieces from background fabric, using pattern piece 6.

8. You will need to make four border strips for each side of the quilt. Each border strip contains two segments.

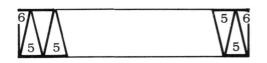

Segment 1: Trees and background using pattern pieces 5 and 6.

Piece 17 tree units in each row.

Segment 2: Trunks and background using pattern pieces 7, 8 and 9. Cut 68 from brown fabric, using pattern piece 8; 64 from background fabric, using pattern piece 9; and 8 pieces from background fabric, using pattern piece 7.

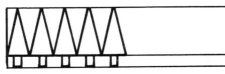

Stitch segment 1 to segment 2, making sure to center each tree trunk.

9. Add a tree border to top and bottom edges of quilt top, with trunk segment next to top of quilt.

10. Piece four corner blocks, using pattern pieces 5 and 8 and corner pieces 10, 11, 12 and 13 in each block.

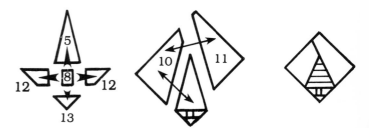

11. Add a corner piece to each end of the remaining border strips, using the diagram as a guide to placement. Sew border strips to side edges of quilt top.

12. Add batting and backing, then quilt or tie. Quilting suggestion: Quilt 1/4" from all seamlines on School House blocks. Quilt down the center from tip through trunk and 1/4" from outer edges of all trees. Quilt 1/4" inside seams on larger trees. Quilt a wavy line on all background and lattice pieces. Add quilting to border 1/4" away from lower edges of trees and trunks. Add a second row of quilting stitches above trees 1" away from previous quilting stitches.

13. Bind with bias strips of green fabric.

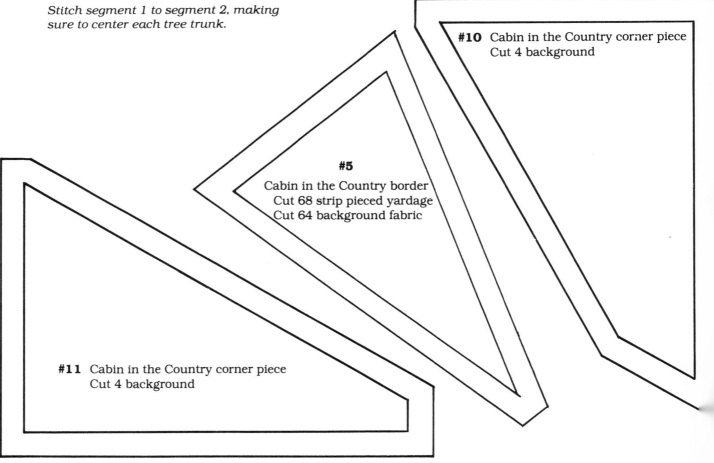

#10 Cabin in the Country corner piece
Cut 4 background

#5
Cabin in the Country border
Cut 68 strip pieced yardage
Cut 64 background fabric

#11 Cabin in the Country corner piece
Cut 4 background

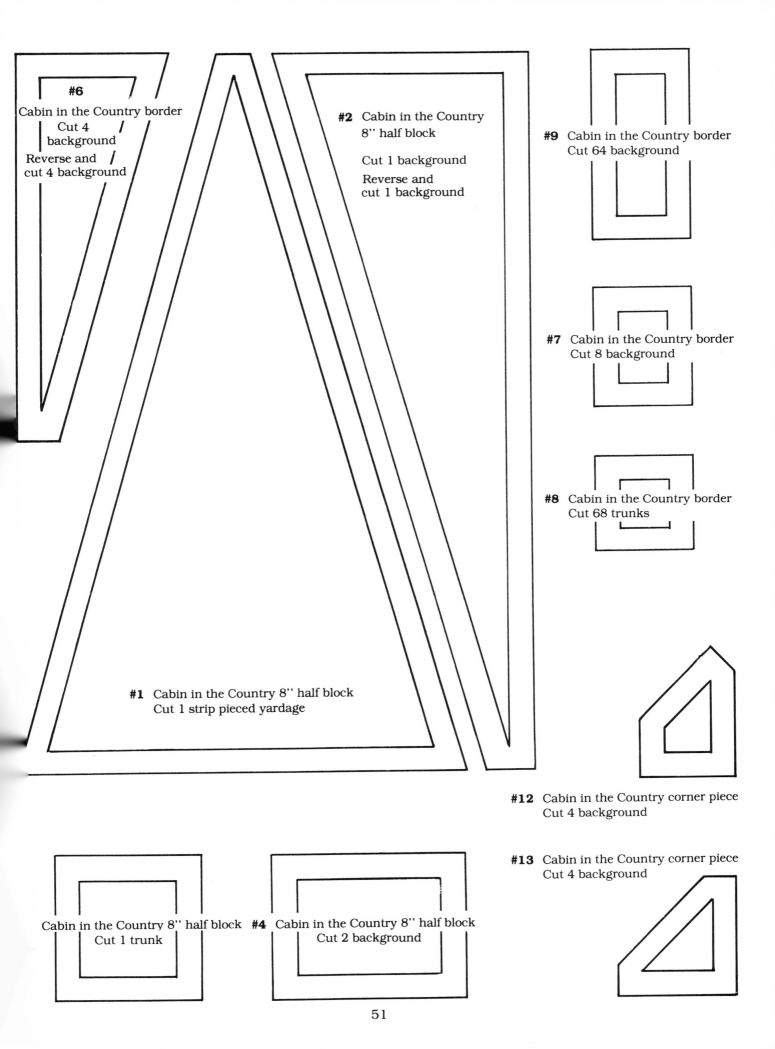

#6
Cabin in the Country border
Cut 4
background

Reverse and
cut 4 background

#2 Cabin in the Country
8'' half block

Cut 1 background

Reverse and
cut 1 background

#9 Cabin in the Country border
Cut 64 background

#7 Cabin in the Country border
Cut 8 background

#8 Cabin in the Country border
Cut 68 trunks

#1 Cabin in the Country 8'' half block
Cut 1 strip pieced yardage

#12 Cabin in the Country corner piece
Cut 4 background

#13 Cabin in the Country corner piece
Cut 4 background

Cabin in the Country 8'' half block
Cut 1 trunk

#4 Cabin in the Country 8'' half block
Cut 2 background

51

Home Sweet Home

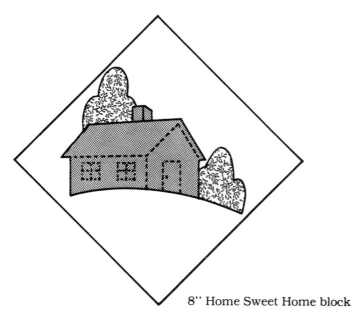

8" Home Sweet Home block

Color:

The colorful appliqued Home Sweet Home quilt, shown in Plate 9 on page 44, served as the inspiration for this quilt block. This version features straight sewn borders rather than an appliqued fence.[9] Bright colors are used for the appliqued and embroidered houses set against a cheerful yellow background. Varying green prints are used for the trees and shrubs. This quilt is unusual because of the diagonal set.

Dimensions: 70" x 93"

Measurements for borders and pattern pieces include 1/4" seam allowances.

Materials: 45"-wide fabric

5 1/2 yds. yellow fabric for background and borders
1 1/2 yds. assorted bright fabrics for houses
   (scraps may be substituted)
3/4 yd. assorted green fabrics for trees and shrubs
4 yds. fabric for backing
1/2 yd. contrasting fabric for binding
81" x 96" Mountain Mist® batting
2 skeins white embroidery floss
1 skein dark embroidery floss

Piecing diagram

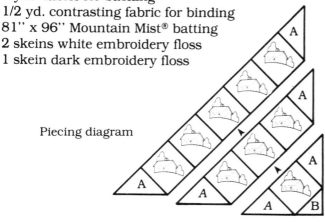

9. *Fences of this type were usually found on coffin quilts or death quilts and were used to enclose graveyards.*

Home Sweet Home 70" x 93"

Directions:

1. This quilt has a simple border with straight sewn corners. From background fabric, cut two 7 1/2" x 79 1/2" strips for length and two 7 1/2" x 71" strips for width.
2. Cut 59 square blocks 8 1/2" x 8 1/2" from background fabric. Cut applique pieces for 59 Home Sweet Home blocks, using the templates provided.
3. Applique 59 Home Sweet Home blocks, using the Paper Patch Applique method described on page 78.
4. Cut 20 set pieces A and four set pieces B from background fabric.
5. Piece Home Sweet Home blocks and set pieces into diagonal rows, using the piecing diagram as a guide.
6. Add straight sewn borders.
7. Add batting and backing, then quilt or tie. Quilting suggestion: Use two strands of embroidery floss and a long quilting stitch through all layers to outline details on houses. Use white embroidery floss on the bright colored houses and dark embroidery floss on white houses. With regular quilting thread, quilt 1/4" from outer edge of houses and strips. Stitch a diagonal grid through the background areas of the quilt, not through the houses. Quilt a cable design around the border.
8. Bind with bias strips of contrasting fabric.

52

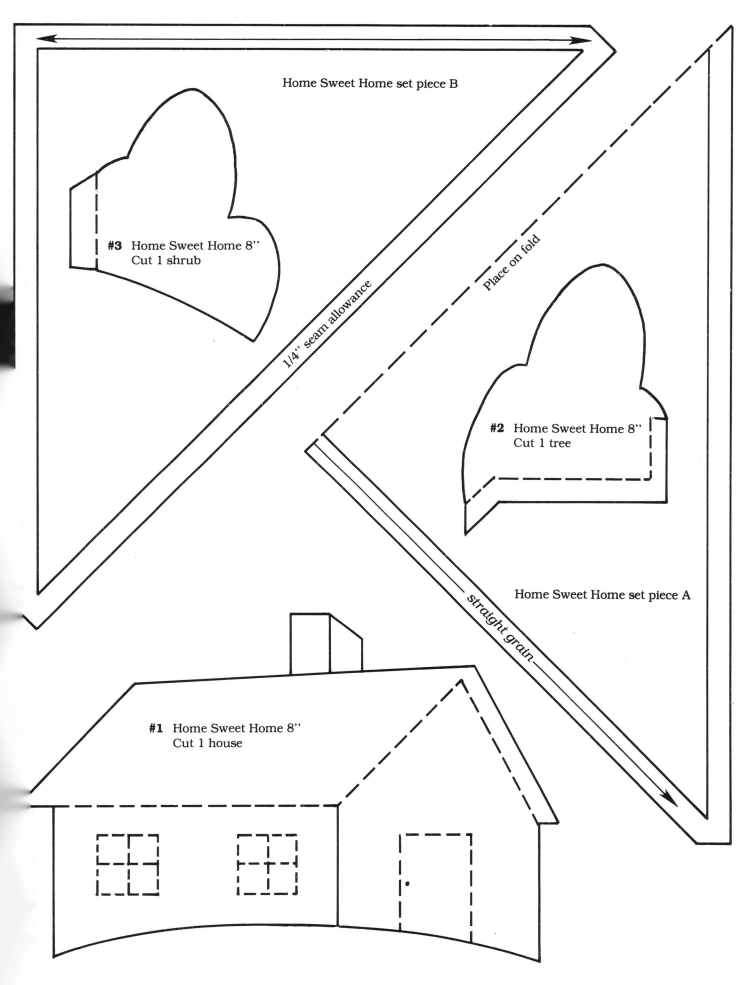

Home Sweet Home set piece B

#3 Home Sweet Home 8''
Cut 1 shrub

1/4'' seam allowance

Place on fold

#2 Home Sweet Home 8''
Cut 1 tree

Home Sweet Home set piece A

straight grain

#1 Home Sweet Home 8''
Cut 1 house

Irish Road to Home Quilt

7 1/2" House block

7 1/2" Double Irish Chain block

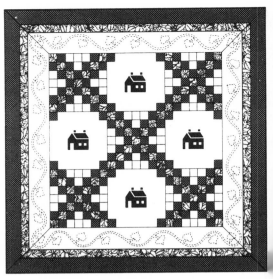
Irish Road to Home 31" x 31"

Color:

This handsome quilt has rust and navy in the patchwork, stenciling design and border, against a muslin background. The vine quilting design adds a touch of charm.

Dimensions: 31" x 31"

Measurements for borders and pattern pieces include 1/4" seam allowances.

Materials: 45"-wide fabric

1/4 yd. muslin for stenciled blocks
   (or purchase four 7 1/2" x 7 1/2" square screen-printed blocks)
1/2 yd. muslin for pieced blocks and first border
3/8 yd. light print fabric for pieced blocks and second border
3/4 yd. dark print fabric for pieced blocks and third border
1 yd. fabric for backing
Mountain Mist® batting, crib size

Directions:

1. Irish Road to Home has multiple borders that are mitered. Cut the border strips and sew them into border units. (See Borders on page 80 and Mitering on page 81.)
   FIRST BORDER: Cut four 3" x 33" strips of muslin.
   SECOND BORDER: Cut four 1 1/2" x 33" strips of light print.
   THIRD BORDER: Cut four 2" x 33" strips of dark print.
2. Cut four 7 1/2" x 7 1/2" square blocks. Stencil a design in the center of each block, using the House Stencil and directions on page 78. Let the stenciling dry. (You may substitute purchased screen-printed blocks.)
3. Construct five pieced blocks, using the pattern piece and the piecing diagram provided. This is the Double Irish Chain pattern.

4. Fold under seam allowances on two sides of fabric squares cut from the pattern piece. Hand applique four fabric squares to each 7 1/2" stenciled square, placing one in each corner of the square and keeping raw edges even.
5. Follow the diagram to set together the four stenciled blocks and the five pieced blocks for the quilt top.
6. Add borders and miter corners.
7. Add batting and backing, then quilt or tie. Quilting suggestion: Quilt 1/4" away from house design. Then quilt a diagonal grid through the center of all pieced blocks, continuing through the stenciled blocks, but not through the houses. Use the vine quilting design on page 82 to quilt the muslin border.
8. Bind with bias strips of the same fabric that was used for outer border.

Piecing diagram

Piece two: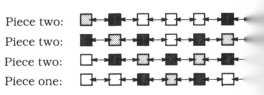
Piece two:
Piece two:
Piece one:

#1 Irish Road to Home
Cut 116 dark fabric
Cut 65 light fabric
Cut 80 muslin

House on the Corner Quilt

6" House block

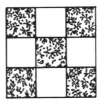

6" Nine Patch

House on the Corner Quilt 40" x 40"

Color:

A dark print combined with muslin highlights the screen-printed blocks.

Dimensions: 40" x 40"

Measurements for borders and pattern pieces include 1/4" seam allowances.

Materials: 45"-wide fabric

3/8 yd. muslin for stenciled blocks
  (or 12 purchased 6 1/2" x 6 1/2" square screen-printed blocks)
5/8 yd. muslin for pieced blocks and first border
1 1/4 yds. print fabric for pieced blocks, second border and bias binding
1 yd. fabric for backing
Mountain Mist® batting, crib size

Directions:

The House on the Corner quilt pictured has multiple mitered borders. Cut the border strips and sew them into border units. (See Borders on page 80 and Mitering on page 81.)
FIRST BORDER: Cut four 2 1/2" x 41" strips of muslin.
SECOND BORDER: Cut four 3 1/2" x 41" strips of print fabric.
Cut 12 blocks 6 1/2" x 6 1/2" square. Stencil a design in the center of each block. Let the stenciling dry. (You may substitute purchased screen-printed blocks or Suzanne's House on page 56.) The alternating patchwork blocks utilize a strip piecing method of construction. If this technique is new to you, read the directions carefully before beginning.

Cut five 2 1/2" x 45" strips of print fabric, cut across the grain. Cut four 2 1/2" x 45" strips of muslin.

B. Using 1/4" seams, piece together two fabric segments, as shown in the diagram. Mark every 2 1/2", then cut apart (see diagram). You will need 26 segments.

C. Using 1/4" seams, piece together one fabric segment, as shown in the diagram. Mark every 2 1/2", then cut apart (see diagram). You will need 13 segments.

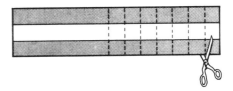

4. Using 1/4" seams, piece together the strip pieced segments to make 13 pieced blocks (see the diagram of a finished block).
5. Follow the quilt diagram to piece the 12 stenciled blocks and 13 pieced blocks together to form the quilt top.
6. Add borders and miter corners.
7. Add batting and backing, then quilt or tie. Quilting suggestion: Quilt a diagonal grid through the center of the pieced blocks. A wide cable design is placed so that quilting appears on both border strips. This quilting design is on page 83.
8. Bind with bias strips of the same fabric that was used for outer border.

Suzanne's House

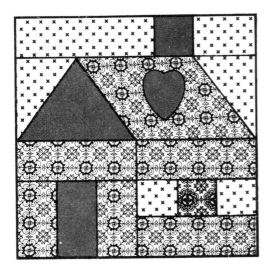

6" Suzanne's House block

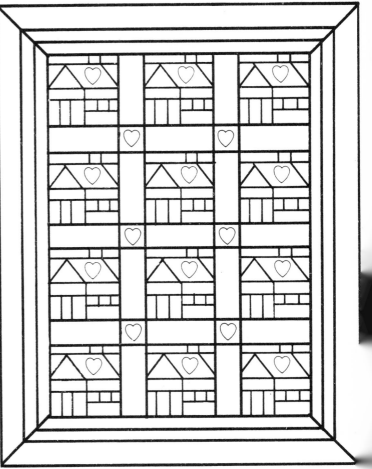

Suzanne's House 30" x 38"

Color:

Houses made from strong primary colors, such as red and blue, set against a print background make a delightful baby quilt, which can later be used as a wall hanging. The red appliqued hearts decorate the roof and lattice squares. Hearts are found on the quilting designs in the border.

Dimensions: 30" x 38"

Measurements for borders and pattern pieces include 1/4" seam allowances.

Materials: 45"-wide fabric

1/2 yd. blue fabric for houses, roofs, lattice squares and first border
3/4 yd. red fabric for roof peak, doors, hearts, chimneys, lattices, third border and binding
1/2 yd. light print for windows, background and second border
1 yd. fabric for backing
Mountain Mist® batting, crib size

Piecing diagram

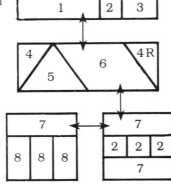

Directions:

1. Suzanne's House has multiple borders that a mitered. Cut the border strips and sew them in border units (see Borders on page 80.)
   FIRST BORDER: Cut two 1 1/2" x 42" strips ar two 1 1/2" x 34" strips from blue.
   SECOND BORDER: Cut two 1 1/2" x 42" stri and two 1 1/2" x 34" strips from light pri
   THIRD BORDER: Cut two 2 1/2" x 42" strips ar two 2 1/2" x 34" strips from red.
2. Cut and piece 12 Suzanne's House blocks.
3. Cut 17 lattice strips 2 1/2" x 6 1/2" and six latt squares 2 1/2" x 2 1/2".
4. Piece three Suzanne's House blocks and two l tice strips into rows.
5. Piece three lattice strips and two lattice squa into rows.
6. Join rows of Suzanne's House blocks and lat strips to rows of lattice strips and squares.
7. Add mitered borders (see Mitering on page 8
8. Applique hearts onto rooftops and lat squares, using the Paper Patch Applique met described on page 78.
9. Add batting and backing, then quilt or Quilting suggestion: Quilt 1/4" away from seamlines and appliqued hearts. On the t border, quilt the heart design on page 82.
10. Bind with bias strips of the same fabric that used for the outer border.

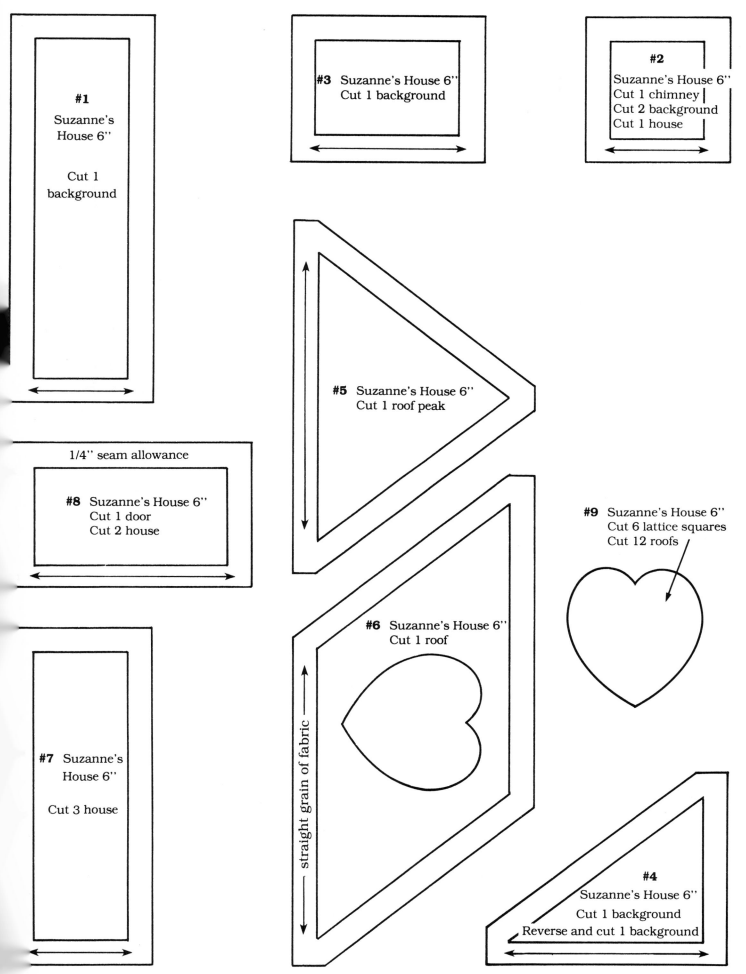

#1
Suzanne's
House 6''

Cut 1
background

#3 Suzanne's House 6''
Cut 1 background

#2
Suzanne's House 6''
Cut 1 chimney
Cut 2 background
Cut 1 house

#5 Suzanne's House 6''
Cut 1 roof peak

1/4'' seam allowance

#8 Suzanne's House 6''
Cut 1 door
Cut 2 house

#9 Suzanne's House 6''
Cut 6 lattice squares
Cut 12 roofs

straight grain of fabric

#6 Suzanne's House 6''
Cut 1 roof

#7 Suzanne's
House 6''

Cut 3 house

#4
Suzanne's House 6''
Cut 1 background
Reverse and cut 1 background

57

Little Love Nest

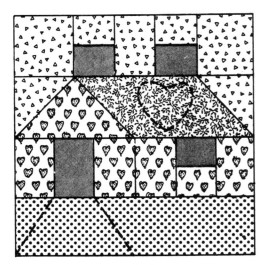

4" Little Love Nest block

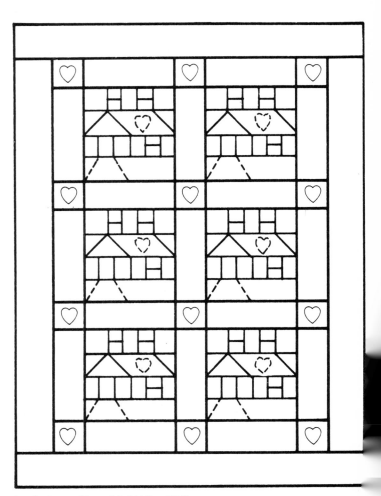

Little Love Nest 14 3/4" x 20"

Color:

Houses made from a tiny heart print fabric are framed by soft pastel prints. Appliqued hearts on the lattice blocks echo the romantic theme.

Dimensions: 14 3/4" x 20"

Measurements for borders and pattern pieces include 1/4" seam allowances.

Materials: 45"-wide fabric

1/4 yd. heart fabric for houses
3/8 yd. blue fabric for sky, border and binding
1/8 yd. lilac fabric for chimneys, doors and windows
1/4 yd. pink fabric for roofs, lattice strips and heart appliques
1/4 yd. green fabric for grass and lattice squares
1/2 yd. fabric for backing
15" x 22" flannel for filler

Directions:

1. This quilt has simple borders with straight sew corners. Cut two 2" x 17 1/2" strips for lengt and two 2" x 15 1/4" strips for width.
2. Cut and piece six Little Love Nest blocks.
3. Cut 17 lattice strips 1 3/4" x 4 1/2" and 12 lattic squares 1 3/4" x 1 3/4".
4. Piece two Little Love Nest blocks and three la tice strips into rows.
5. Piece three lattice squares and two lattice strip into rows.
6. Join rows of lattice squares and strips to rows Little Love Nest blocks and lattice strips.
7. Add borders.
8. Applique hearts onto lattice squares, using t Paper Patch Applique method described on pa 78.
9. Add flannel as a filler and backing, then quilt tie. Quilting suggestion: Quilt a heart design each roof and a double heart design in latt squares. Quilt 1/8" away from edges of ap qued hearts and "in the ditch" around ea block. A pathway to each house is quilted. Qui heart design in the border. The quilting desi for hearts and double hearts are on page 82.
10. Bind with bias strips of border fabric.

Piecing diagram

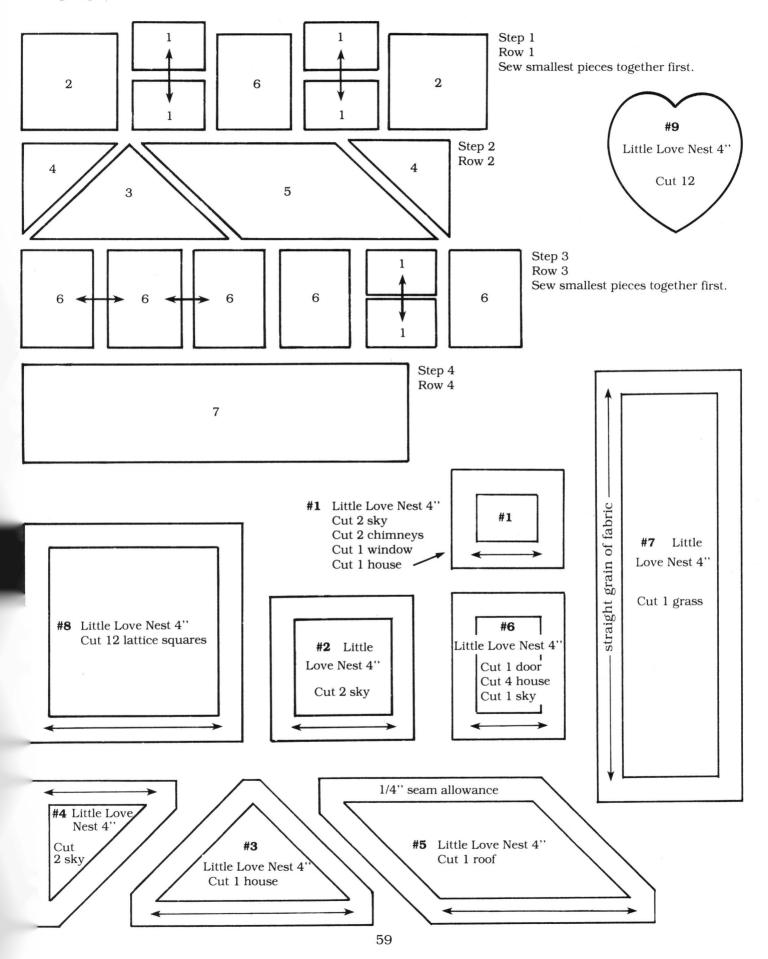

Step 1
Row 1
Sew smallest pieces together first.

Step 2
Row 2

Step 3
Row 3
Sew smallest pieces together first.

Step 4
Row 4

#9
Little Love Nest 4''

Cut 12

#1 Little Love Nest 4''
Cut 2 sky
Cut 2 chimneys
Cut 1 window
Cut 1 house

#1

#7   Little
Love Nest 4''

Cut 1 grass

straight grain of fabric

#8 Little Love Nest 4''
Cut 12 lattice squares

#2   Little
Love Nest 4''

Cut 2 sky

#6
Little Love Nest 4''

Cut 1 door
Cut 4 house
Cut 1 sky

1/4'' seam allowance

#4 Little Love
Nest 4''

Cut
2 sky

#3
Little Love Nest 4''
Cut 1 house

#5 Little Love Nest 4''
Cut 1 roof

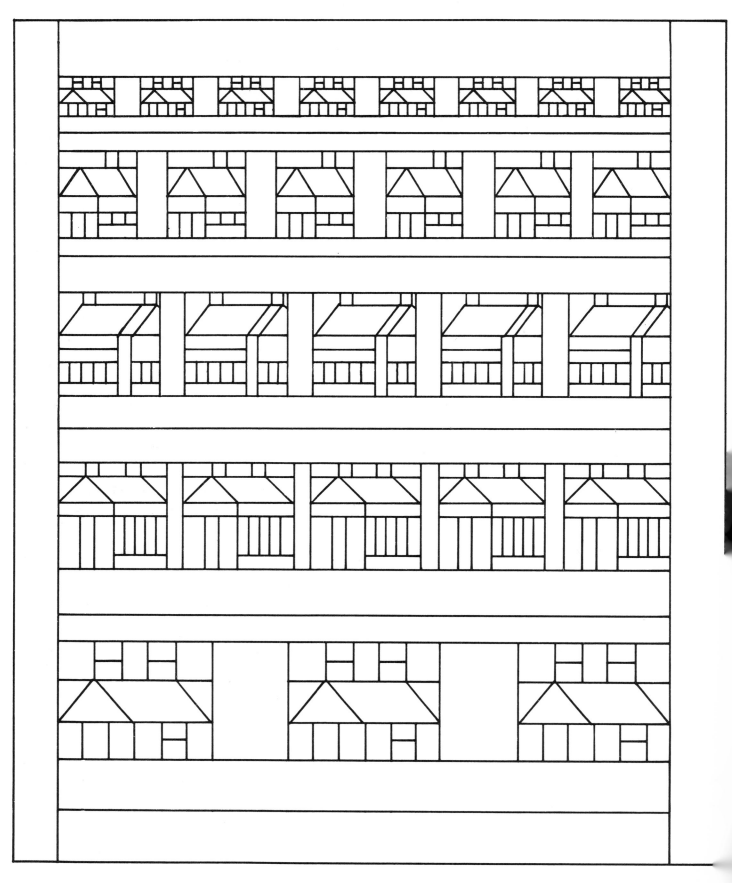

Housing Projects 55'' x 63 1/2''

Housing Projects Sampler

Color:

Different pastel colors are used for each row of houses with a deep geometric print used for the roofs and doors. A sense of unity prevails in this strippy style sampler quilt with the use of the same rose fabric for all the chimneys and muslin for all the windows. In addition, the muted blue for the sky and green for the grass are the right intensity to contrast with the pastel houses. The coloration of this quilt was suggested by the folk song "Little Boxes:"[10]

> "Little boxes on the hillside,
> Little boxes made of ticky tacky
> Little boxes on the hillside,
> Little boxes all the same
> There's a green one and a pink one
> And a blue one and a yellow one
> And they're all made out of ticky tacky
> And they all look just the same."

Dimensions: 55" x 63 1/2"

Measurements for borders and pattern pieces include 1/4" seam allowances.

Materials: 45"-wide fabric

1/4 yd. light blue fabric for 4" Little Love Nest houses
1/8 yd. deep blue fabric for 4" Little Love Nest roofs and doors
3/8 yd. pink fabric for 6" Suzanne's House blocks
1/8 yd. deep pink fabric for 6" Suzanne's House block roofs and doors
3/8 yd. coral fabric for 8" House blocks
1/8 yd. rust fabric for 8" House block roofs
1/2 yd. mauve fabric for 8" School House blocks
1/8 yd. deep mauve fabric for 8" School House block roofs and doors
3/8 yd. light green fabric for House on a Hill blocks
1/8 yd. deep green fabric for House on a Hill roofs and doors
1/8 yd. rose fabric for all chimneys
1/4 yd. muslin for all windows and contrasting strips in 8" House blocks.
2 yds. blue fabric for sky, background and borders
1 1/2 yds. green fabric for grass
3 3/4 yds. fabric for backing and binding
72" x 90" Mountain Mist® batting

Directions:

This sampler quilt is made "strippy style," using five patterns previously introduced. For all blocks, do not use any grass pattern pieces. The unity of the quilt and the strong horizontal movement is achieved by stitching lattice between the houses, and then adding one continuous strip to represent grass.

2. This quilt has simple borders with straight sewn corners. Cut two 5" x 63 1/2" strips for length and two 5" x 46 1/2" strips for width.
3. Cut and piece eight Little Love Nest blocks, using pattern pieces on pages 58-59.
4. Cut seven 2 1/2" x 3 1/2" lattice pieces. Piece lattice between all Little Love Nest blocks.
5. Add top border strip above row of Little Love Nest blocks. Add 1 1/2" x 46 1/2" strip of green fabric for grass below houses.
6. Cut and piece six Suzanne's House blocks, referring to the piecing diagram on page 56.
7. Cut five 2 1/2" x 6 1/2" lattice pieces. Piece lattice between Suzanne's House blocks.
8. Cut a 1 1/2" x 46 1/2" blue strip of sky and add above houses. Add 1 1/2" x 46 1/2" strip of green fabric for grass below houses.
9. Cut and piece five House blocks (8" size), using the pattern pieces on pages 36 and 37, omitting pattern pieces 14, 15 and 16.
10. Cut four 2" x 8 1/2" lattice pieces. Piece lattice between House blocks.
11. Cut a 3" x 46 1/2" blue strip of sky and add above the Houses. Cut a 3" x 46 1/2" green strip of grass and add below these Houses.
12. Cut and piece five School House blocks (8" size), using the pattern pieces on page 40.
13. Cut four 2" x 8 1/2" lattice pieces. Piece lattice between School House blocks.
14. Cut a 3" x 46 1/2" blue strip of sky and add above the School House blocks. Cut 4" x 46 1/2" strip of green grass and add below the School House blocks.
15. Cut and piece three House on a Hill blocks, using the pattern pieces on pages 15, 16 and 17.
16. Cut two 5 1/2" x 9 1/2" lattice pieces. Piece lattice between House on a Hill blocks.
17. Cut a 2 1/2" x 46 1/2" blue strip of sky and add to top of House on a Hill blocks.
18. Cut a 4 1/2" x 46 1/2" green strip of grass and add to lower edge of House on a Hill blocks. Then add lower border strip.
19. Piece the rows of house blocks together, using the following order from top to bottom of quilt: Little Love Nest, Suzanne's House, House, School House and House on a Hill.
20. Add side border strips.
21. Add batting and backing, then quilt or tie. Quilting suggestion: Quilt a grid of hanging diamonds on quilt top, using the diagonal line of the House on a Hill roof to determine placement. Surround the houses with a quilted tulip design on the border.
22. Bind with bias strips of green fabric.

10. © *Malvina Reynolds, 1962, Schroder Music Company.*

Projects

Ruffled Pillows

Finished Size: Can be made in a variety of sizes

Materials:

Pillows are an excellent way to display house blocks. The amount of fabric needed is dependent upon pillow size. An 18" x 18" ruffled pillow requires approximately 1 1/4 yards of fabric for the pillow back and ruffle. Usually 1/4 yard of each print will make a house block for the pillow front. Pillow may be stuffed with Mountain Mist® Fiberloft® stuffing or a purchased pillow form.

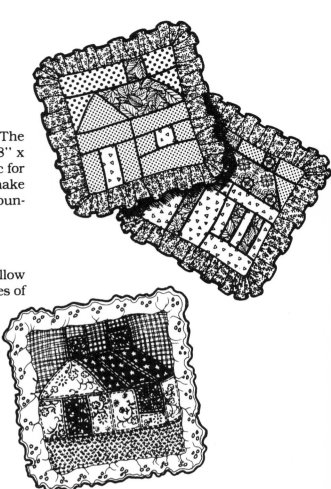

Pillow Top

1. Determine the finished size of the pillow. Cut out the pillow back and batting, adding 1/4" seam allowances on all sides of the pillow.
2. Piece block for pillow front.
3. Add straight sewn or mitered borders if desired.

Ruffle

1. Making fabric ruffles is easy to do and adds such a nice finish to pillows. You can make a folded or hemmed ruffle.
2. Figure the length of the ruffle to equal twice the length of the area to which it will be sewn.
3. Select the width of the finished ruffle. If making a folded ruffle measure twice the finished width, plus 1/4" for seam allowances. For a hemmed ruffle, measure the width, plus 1" for the hemmed edge and the seam allowance.
4. After determining the length and width of the ruffle, cut a strip (or strips) of fabric to equal those measurements. Seam the strips together to make a ruffle the required length.
5. You may purchase gathered trim to add to the pillow top in place of or in addition to a fabric ruffle.
6. To make a folded ruffle, fold the ruffle lengthwise with the wrong sides of the fabric together and steam press the length of the ruffle. Sew a gathering stitch along the raw edges of the ruffle. Gather that edge to the required length.
7. To make a hemmed ruffle, press one edge of the ruffle under and machine hem. Sew a gathering stitch along the remaining raw edge of the ruffle. Gather that edge to the required length.
8. Gathered trims and ruffles are attached in the same way. With the right side of the trim or ruffle facing the right side of the pillow front, pin in place with the raw edges even and the finished edge of trim or ruffle toward the center of the pillow front. Extra trim or ruffle should be eased into the corners, and outer edges should be carefully pinned so they will not be caught in the stitching.

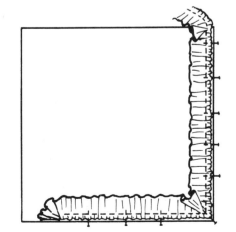

9. Take time to hide the beginning and end of the trim or ruffle. Do not start at the corners of a square piece; instead, overlap along a straight edge.
10. Adjust the gathers to fit and baste the trim or ruffle in place. If using two different sized ruffles, baste the narrower one in place first.
11. Pin the pillow back to the pillow front with the right sides together. Stitch in a 1/4" seam, leaving an opening for turning.
12. Turn the pillow cover through the opening. If the edge of the trim or ruffle has been caught in the seam, carefully open the seam in this area. Reposition the trim or ruffle. Stuff lightly with Mountain Mist® Fiberloft® stuffing. Slip stitch the opening closed.

Alternate Finishing Techniques

There are other options for finishing pillows. You can make a lapped back which allows a pillow form to slip easily in and out. You can even make your own pillow form from batting and polyester stuffing.

1. A lapped-back pillow cover requires two pillow back pieces. Cut each one the same width as the pillow front. Adjust the length to equal one-half the pillow back length plus 2". Sew a narrow hem along one long edge of each pillow back piece.
2. Follow the diagram for the correct placement of the pillow pieces.
3. Stitch 1/2" from all edges. Trim the corners and turn to the right side.
4. Insert a purchased pillow form or make your own. To make a pillow form, cut two pieces of batting the desired finished size of the pillow, adding 1/2" to both the length and width measurements. Stitch the batting together in a 1/4" seam, leaving a small opening through which to stuff. Do not turn the pillow form. Stuff with polyester stuffing and slip stitch the opening closed.

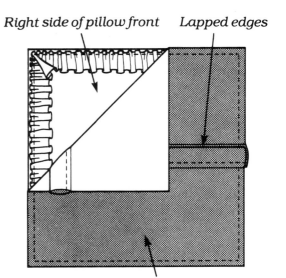

Right side of pillow front   Lapped edges

Wrong side of pillow back

63

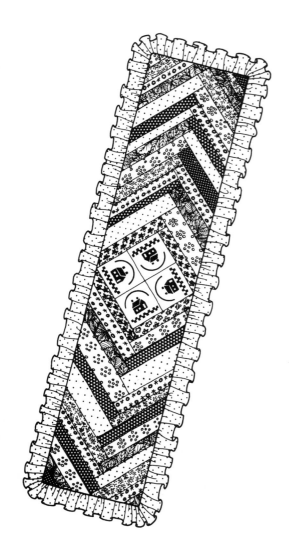

Table Runner

Finished Size: 4 1/2" x 50"

Materials:

12" x 48" piece needlepunch or batting
Four 4" Little Love Nest blocks
Assorted fabric strips for strip quilting, cut 1 1/4" to 2 1/2" wide
2 yds. print fabric for table runner backing and ruffle

Directions:

1. Construct four 4" Little Love Nest blocks, using templates on page 59. You may substitute purchased screen-printed blocks, each cut to a 4 1/2" square.
2. Stitch the four pieced or screen-printed blocks together, using the diagram as a placement guide. Baste in place, centering blocks diagonally on the needlepunch.
3. Randomly select fabric strips to strip quilt around center motif. Using a rotary cutter and straight edge, cut strips 1 1/4" to 2 1/2" wide across the grain of fabric.
   - A. Place the first strip right side down along any edge of motif. Stitch in a 1/4" seam. Flip fabric so that right side faces up and finger press in place. Trim end of strip even with edge of center motif.
   - B. Place another fabric strip right side down along the adjacent edge of the motif and the raw edge of the first strip. Stitch in a 1/4" seam. Flip fabric so right side is up and finger press in place. Trim end of strip even with edge of center motif.
   - C. Repeat this procedure along the remaining two edges of the motif.
   - D. Continue to strip quilt in this manner, working from the center to the edges of the needlepunch. When all the needlepunch has been covered, steam press and trim the edges.
4. To make the ruffle, cut seven 3 1/2" x 45" strips from print fabric. With the wrong sides of the fabrics together, sew the ends together and press seam allowances flat. Sew a narrow hem on one edge of the ruffle. Run a gathering stitch along the other edge of the ruffle. Pull the thread and adjust the gathers to fit the outer edges of the table runner. With the right sides together, pin the ruffle to the table runner front, keeping the raw edges even and placing the finished edge of the ruffle toward the center of the table runner. Baste in place.
5. Stitch the table runner back to the front, right sides together, in a 1/4" seam. Be sure to leave an opening for turning.
6. Clip the corners and turn the table runner to the right side. Steam press and slip stitch the opening closed.

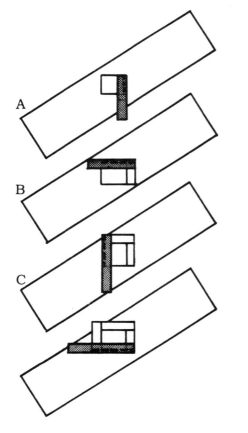

Potholder

Finished Size: 8" x 8"

Materials:

Two 8 1/2" x 8 1/2" squares needlepunch
Two 8 1/2" x 8 1/2" fabric squares for front and backing
2" double fold bias tape
1 skein white embroidery floss
Fabric scraps for Home Sweet Home block

Directions:

1. Cut and paper piece an 8" Home Sweet Home block, using templates on page 53. Applique to 8 1/2" x 8 1/2" fabric square for potholder front. Follow Paper Patch Applique directions on page 78.
2. Baste needlepunch to wrong side of potholder front and backing.
3. Stitch together open edges of the bias tape. Fold raw edges together and pin in one corner of the potholder to serve as a loop. Baste in place.
4. Pin potholder front to backing with right sides together. Stitch in 1/4" seam, leaving an opening for turning.
5. Clip corners, trim the seams, and turn the potholder to the right side.
6. Steam press. With two strands of embroidery floss, add decorative quilting lines to the Home Sweet Home block.
7. Stitch the opening closed and topstitch 1/4" from finished edges.

Kitchen Towel

Finished Size: 18" long

Materials:

4" Little Love Nest block
Kitchen towel, cut in half lengthwise
1/4 yd. fabric for flap and backing
4 1/2" x 8 1/2" piece needlepunch

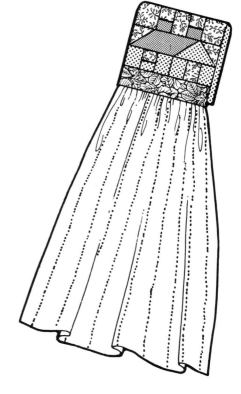

Directions:

1. Piece one Little Love Nest block, using templates on page 59.
2. Cut a 4 1/2" x 4 1/2" fabric square for flap. With right sides together, stitch in a 1/4" seam to upper edge of Little Love Nest block.
3. Cut a 4 1/2" x 8 1/2" piece of backing.
4. With right sides together, stitch backing to block and flap along side and upper edges in a 1/4" seam. Clip corners and turn to outside. Press.
5. Gather the cut edge of the towel to fit the lower edge of the Little Love Nest block.
6. With right sides together, pin the towel to the open edge of the block. Sew a 1/4" seam. Press.
7. Turn the backing edge under 1/4" and pin in place. Stitch closed. Press.
8. Center a buttonhole near the edge of the flap. Fold in half to determine placement, then sew a button on the backing.
9. To hang, button over a door or drawer handle in the kitchen.

Placemat

Finished Size: 12" x 18"

Materials:

Three 4" Little Love Nest blocks
1/2 yd. fabric for strips and placemat backing
12 1/2" x 18 1/2" piece needlepunch

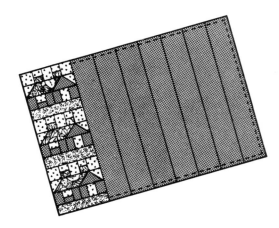

Directions:

1. Piece three Little Love Nest blocks, using templates on page 59. Stitch together in a column. Pin in place on left side of 12 1/2" x 18 1/2" needlepunch.
2. Cut seven 2 1/2" x 14" fabric strips.
3. Strip quilt by placing first strip of fabric on pieced blocks, with right sides together and raw edges even. Stitch in a 1/4" seam.
4. Flip fabric so that right side is up and finger press in place.
5. Place another fabric strip on top of the previously sewn strip, with right sides together and raw edges even. Stitch in a 1/4" seam, then flip fabric so that right side is up. Finger press in place.
6. Continue this procedure until all seven fabric strips have been sewn to the needlepunch.
7. Steam press, using a very damp cloth. In case batting has become distorted, use a rotary cutter and straight edge to trim it to the original 12 1/2" x 18 1/2".
8. Cut a 12 1/2" x 18 1/2" piece of fabric for backing. Pin backing to quilted needlepunch with right sides together.
9. Stitch in a 1/4" seam, leaving an opening for turning.
10. Clip corners, trim the seams and turn the placemat to the right side.
11. Steam press.
12. Stitch the opening closed; then topstitch 1/4" from finished edges.

House Sampler

Finished Size: 6" x 6"

Materials:

4" Little Love Nest block
10" x 10" piece 18 count Aida cloth
1 skein embroidery floss
6" x 6" wooden frame

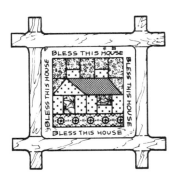

Directions:

1. Piece one Little Love Nest block, using templates on page 59
2. Press under 1/4" on raw edges of block.
3. Position block in center of 10" x 10" Aida cloth. Blind stitch in place.
4. Using the chart on page 67 as a guide, work "Bless This House" motif along each edge of quilt block, using one strand of embroidery floss.
5. Trim to 6" x 6" and mount in a 6" x 6" wooden frame.

66

Tote Bag

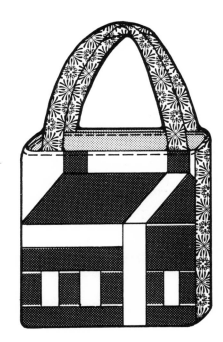

Finished Size: 12" square

Materials:

Two 12" House blocks
1/8 yd. prequilted fabric
1/2 yd. coordinating fabric for the lining and handle

Directions:

1. For the front and back of the tote bag, construct two 12" House blocks, using the 12" pattern of your choice.
2. Cut a 3" x 37" gusset from the prequilted fabric.
3. With right sides together, stitch the gusset to the tote front, side and bottom edges in a 1/4" seam.
4. Stitch the tote back to the gusset in the same manner. Turn to the right side and press.
5. Cut two 3" x 18" fabric strips for the tote handles. Fold each in half lengthwise with the right sides together; stitch along the long edges in a 1/4" seam. Turn to the right side and press.
6. Pin the handles to the upper edges of the tote front and back, centering each end of each handle 2" from the side edges. Baste in place.
7. Cut two 12 1/2" x 12 1/2" squares from the lining fabric for the front and back lining. Cut a 3" x 37" piece of fabric for the gusset lining. Construct the lining in the same manner as the outside of the tote. Use 1/4" seams to stitch the tote front and back lining to the gusset lining. Press, but do not turn to the right side.
8. Slip the tote inside the lining; with right sides together, pin together along the upper edges. Sew in a 1/4" seam, stitching in the handles and leaving an opening for turning.
9. Turn the tote to the right side and adjust the lining inside the tote. Slip stitch the opening closed.
10. Topstitch 1/4" away from the upper edges.

Cross-stitch chart

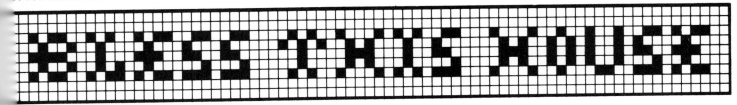

Use the example below to determine size.

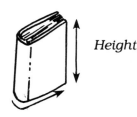

Height

Length edge to edge when closed

Book Cover

Finished Size: Varies to fit different book sizes

Materials:

8" School House or 10" House block
Needlepunch
3/4 yd. fabric for strips, flaps and lining

Directions:

1. Construct an 8" School House block, using templates on page 40, or a 10" House block, using templates on pages 36 and 37.
2. Cut pieces of needlepunch and lining, adding 1" to the book dimensions to allow for batting fullness and for seam allowances.
3. Cut two end flaps, each 4" wide and the height of the book plus 1".
4. Place the House or School House block on the batting, positioning it so block will be centered on the front of the book cover. Baste in place.
5. Cut several 2"-wide fabric strips across the grain. Strip quilt from the top of the block to the top edge of the batting. Repeat for bottom of the block. See directions 3-6 on page 66 for strip quilting directions.
6. Strip quilt from both sides of the block to the batting edges.
7. When all the batting is covered, steam press. Clip excess fabric and trim to the original dimension in case the batting has been stretched.
8. Sew a narrow hem along one edge of the flap pieces. Layer pieces: quilted batting right side up; hemmed flap pieces right side down (with raw edges even and hemmed edge toward center); lining right side down.
9. Stitch along all outside edges in a 1/4" seam, leaving a 3" opening along the top for turning. Clip corners and turn so that the flaps and lining are on the inside. Press and stitch the opening closed. The book cover is now ready to slip on a notebook, cookbook, photograph album or other book.

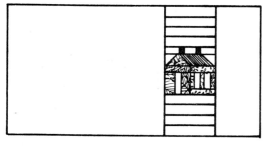

Flap *Flap*

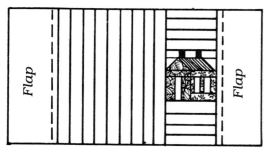

Flap *Lining* *Flap*

Inside of book cover

Purse with Quilted Flap

Finished Size: 12" square plus shoulder strap

Materials:

3/4 yd. sturdy fabric such as denim, corduroy, poplin or sailcloth
1/2 yd. calico for lining and ruffle
12" House on a Hill block

Directions:

1. Construct a 12" House on a Hill block, using templates on pages 15 and 16.
2. If hand quilting, back with backing and batting; hand quilt 1/4" away from all seams.
3. Cut two 3" x 36" strips of sturdy fabric for the shoulder strap. With the right sides together, stitch along the two long sides in a 1/4" seam. Turn and press.
4. Cut two 3" x 45" calico strips for the ruffled trim. With the right sides together, sew a 1/4" seam along the 3" edge. Press the seam flat.
5. Fold the fabric in half lengthwise with the wrong sides together and stitch across each end.
6. Trim the corners, turn and press.
7. Run a long gathering stitch 1/4" from the raw edges of the fabric. Pull thread to gather.
8. Adjust the gathers and pin to the sides and bottom of the quilted block, keeping the raw edges even. Baste in place.
9. Cut a 12 1/2" x 12 1/2" calico square for the purse flap backing.
10. With the right sides together, sew the quilted block to the calico fabric backing in a 1/4" seam along the side and bottom edges. Be careful not to catch the ruffle in the seam. Turn to the right side and press. Baste the upper edge closed with a 1/4" seam. Topstitch 1/4" from the finished edge.
11. Cut a 12 1/2" x 24 1/2" piece of sturdy fabric for the purse and a 12 1/2" x 24 1/2" piece of calico for the lining.
12. With the right sides together, fold the purse fabric in half lengthwise and stitch along both side edges in a 1/4" seam. Repeat for lining fabric.
13. Turn the purse piece right side out. With the right sides together, pin the finished purse flap to the purse. Center the shoulder straps above the side seams. They are attached to the right side of the back of the purse, not the flap side (see diagram).
14. Leaving the lining piece inside out, place the purse with the straps and flap inside the lining piece. Match the side seams and keep the raw edges even. Pin in place. Stitch along this top edge through all thicknesses, leaving a small opening between the two straps for turning.
5. Turn to the right side. Press the opening closed. Machine stitch along the top of this back purse edge. Push the lining down inside the purse and adjust the bottom corners so they meet. Turn the purse and lining to the inside. Fold the bottom corner to make a triangle. Stitch across. Do the same on the other corner (see diagram).

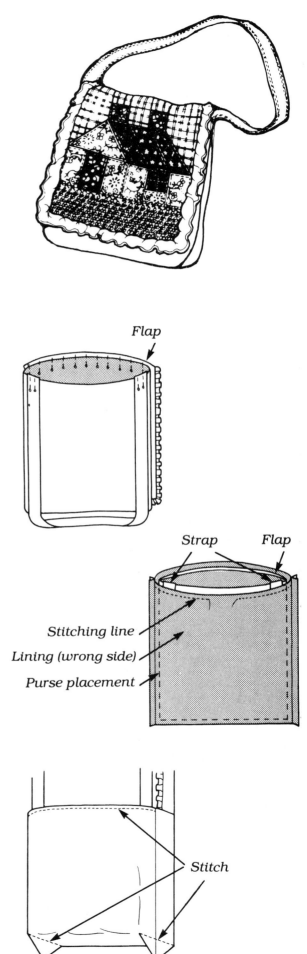

Flap

Strap   *Flap*

Stitching line
Lining (wrong side)
Purse placement

Stitch

Bib Apron

Materials:

1 1/4 yds. print fabric
12" House on a Hill block, quilted

Directions:

1. Cut the fabric for the apron, using the diagramed specifications.
2. For the apron bib, construct and quilt a 12" House on a Hill block, using templates on pages 15 and 16.
3. For the ruffle, seam together two 3" x 30" fabric strips along the 3" edge. Press flat. Fold the fabric in half lengthwise with the wrong sides together. Press. Run a long gathering stitch 1/4" from the raw edges of the fabric. Pull the thread to gather. Adjust the gathers and pin to the top and side edges of the bib apron. Baste in place.
4. For the apron strap, fold one 3" x 30" piece of fabric in half lengthwise with the right sides together. Sew the long edges in a 1/4" seam. Clip the corners, turn and press.
5. Pin the strap to the top of the apron bib, keeping the raw edges even. Adjust the length of the strap to fit comfortably around your neck. Pin in place.
6. Pin the bib facing to the front of the bib with the right sides together. Sew along the top and side edges in a 1/4" seam, being sure to catch in strap edges. Reinforce the stitching over the straps.
7. Trim the corners, turn to the right side and press. Baste the lower edges together.
8. Optional topstitching may be added 1/4" from the finished edges.
9. To make the ties, cut two 4" x 22" fabric strips. Fold in half lengthwise with the right sides together. Sew the long edge and across the bottom in a 1/4" seam. Trim the corners, turn and press.
10. For the waistband, use the other 3" x 30" piece of fabric; cut it slightly shorter than your waist measurement. Fold in half lengthwise with the right sides together, placing a tie in each end and keeping the raw edges even. Stitch the ends. Turn to the right side.
11. Machine or hand hem the side and bottom edges of the apron skirt.
12. Sew a long gathering stitch across the waist edge of the apron skirt. Adjust the gathers so that the apron skirt fits on the waistband. With the right sides together, sew one edge of the waistband to the apron in a 1/4" seam, being careful not to catch the other waistband edge in the seam. Press the seam allowance toward the waistband. Press a 1/4" hem on the remaining waistband edge and pin in place on the inside of the apron. Press.
13. Center the apron bib on the waistband with the bib raw edge behind the waistband. Pin in place. Topstitch the apron waistband 1/4" from all edges. This will tack down the facing on the apron waistband and also attach the bib to the apron skirt.
14. Hand stitch the waistband facing in place.

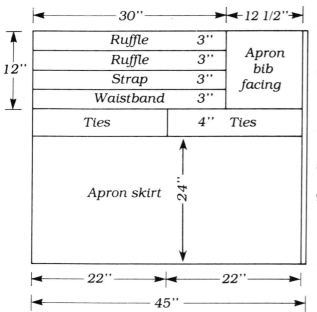

← 30" →			← 12 1/2" →
Ruffle	3"		Apron bib facing
Ruffle	3"		
Strap	3"		
Waistband	3"		
Ties		4" Ties	
Apron skirt (24")			

← 22" → ← 22" →
← 45" →

12"

Pinafore

Finished Size: Fits chest sizes 30" - 36"

Materials:

12" House on a Hill block, quilted
1 yd. coordinating fabric

Directions:

1. Cut the fabric for the pinafore, using the specifications in the diagram.
2. Piece and quilt a 12" House on a Hill block, using templates on pages 15 and 16.
3. Cut two 5" x 10" fabric strips for shoulder straps. Fold each piece in half lengthwise, right sides together. Stitch in a 1/4" seam. Turn to right side and press. Topstitch 1/8" from edge and then topstitch again 1/4" from first stitching.
4. With right sides together and raw edges even, pin straps to quilted House on a Hill block along upper edge. Place 12 1/2" x 12 1/2" facing over this, right sides together. Stitch around sides and across top in a 1/4" seam, being sure to catch in raw edges of straps. Reinforce straps with another row of stitching.
5. Trim corners, turn and press. Topstitch 1/8" from finished edges.
6. Cut two 12 1/2" x 12 1/2" pieces of fabric for pinafore back. Attach remaining raw edges of straps to the top of the pinafore back in the same manner as for pinafore front. Stitch backs together in a 1/4" seam, being sure to catch in raw edges of straps. Reinforce straps with another row of stitching.
7. Trim corners, turn and press. Topstitch 1/8" from finished edges.
8. For pinafore skirt, cut two pieces of fabric 22" wide by 15" long. With right sides together, stitch skirt side seams in a 1/2" seam, ending stitching 4" from top edge. Press seams open. Along the unstitched portion of each skirt side seam, stitch close to the edge, down one side and up the other side. Stitch again 3/8" from first stitching, turning square corners at the bottom of each opening.
9. To hem bottom edge of pinafore skirt, turn under a 1/2" hem, folding under the raw edge. Stitch on wrong side, being sure to stitch down hem edge. Topstitch on the right side close to the folded edge.
10. Sew a row of gathering stitches across the top of the front and back skirt panels. Adjust gathers to fit. With right sides together and raw edges even, pin front skirt panel to front bib section. Pin other skirt panel to back bib. Side edges should be aligned. Stitch. Press seam toward bib.
11. For waistline ties, fold two 3" x 34" fabric strips in half lengthwise, right sides together. Stitch along all edges, leaving an opening for turning. Turn and press. Lay one tie piece over the seamline that joins the pinafore bib and skirt, extending an equal amount of tie on each side. Pin in place. Topstitch close to the edge across the top of tie, around the end, and back across the tie and pinafore, stitching through all thicknesses. Topstitch again 3/8" from the edge. Repeat to attach other tie.
12. Pinafore is worn by slipping over head and tying loosely on each side.

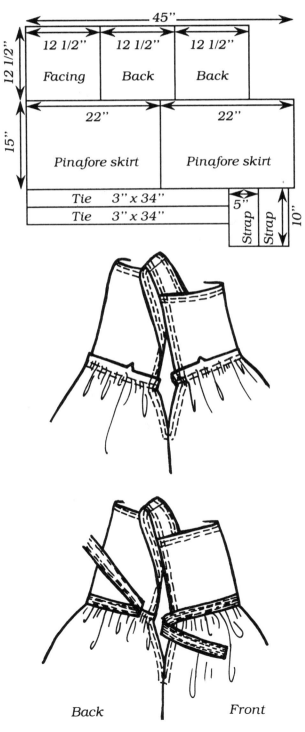

Back　　　　*Front*

71

Magazine Holder

Finished Size: 12" x 46"

Materials:

Three completed 12" House blocks
24 1/2" x 50" piece canvas
12 1/2" x 37 1/2" piece Mountain Mist® batting
12 1/2" x 37 1/2" piece fabric for backing
1" wooden dowel, 14" long
12 1/2" x 37 1/2" piece muslin

Directions:

1. Cut three 12 1/2" x 12 1/2" squares from batting, muslin and backing fabric.
2. Make three House blocks, using the 12" pattern of your choice. Layer pieced House blocks with batting and muslin squares; quilt by hand or machine.
3. With right sides together, pin a quilted House block to a backing fabric square. Sew a 1/4" seam around all sides of the block, leaving an opening for turning. Repeat with other two House blocks.
4. Clip corners, turn and press. Stitch opening closed.
5. Fold canvas in half, forming a 12 1/4" x 50" rectangle. Sew a 1/4" side seam. Press and position this seam down the center back.
6. Sew a 1/4" seam across the bottom of the canvas. Clip corners, turn and press.
7. Fold the canvas top 4" toward the back. Pin in place. Double stitch along the edge to form a 3 1/2" casing.
8. Position the three House blocks on the front of the canvas. Baste in place.
9. Topstitch 1/8" from edge around three sides of each block to form a pocket for books or magazines.
10. Insert a 1" wooden dowel rod through the casing. This holder can be attached to wall studs or hung with a rope and a dowel.

Glossary of Quilt Construction[11]

Supplies

Tools

Sewing Machine

It needn't be fancy. All you need is an evenly locking straight stitch. Whatever kind of sewing machine you have, get to know it and how it runs. If it needs servicing, have it done, or get out the manual and do it yourself. Replace the old needle with a new one. Often, if your machine has a zigzag stitch, it will have a throat plate with an oblong hole for the needle to pass through. You might want to replace this plate with one that has a little round hole for straight stitching. This will help eliminate problems you might have with the edges of fabrics being fed into the hole by the action of the feed dogs.

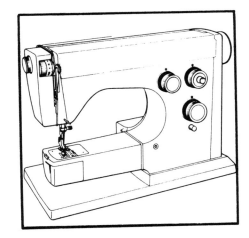

Scissors

Two types of scissors are required: one for paper, and a good sharp pair for cutting fabric only. A little pair for snipping threads might also be helpful. If your fabric scissors are dull, have them sharpened. If they are close to "dead," invest in a new pair; it's worth it.

Ruler

A clear plastic ruler, 2" wide and 18" long with a red 1/8" grid on it, is one tool I could not live without. Use it for making templates, measuring and marking borders, and marking quilting lines. If your local quilt shop doesn't carry them, try a stationery store or any place that carries drafting or art supplies. Another useful tool is a 12" plastic 45°/90° right angle.

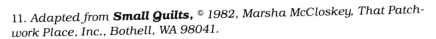

11. Adapted from **Small Quilts,** © 1982, Marsha McCloskey, That Patch-work Place, Inc., Bothell, WA 98041.

Rotary Cutter and Mat

A rotary cutter and mat will save a great deal of time cutting strips for strip quilting and bias strips for binding.

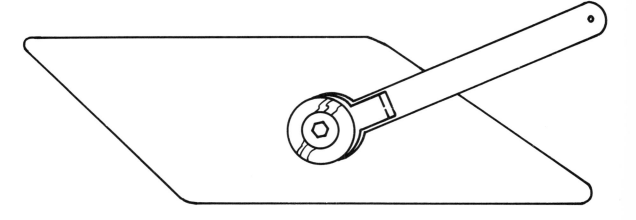

Template Material

1/4" graph paper, lightweight posterboard or plastic and a glue stick.

Seam Ripper

I always keep one handy, just in case.

Needles

You'll need an assortment of Sharps for handwork, and quiltin needles (Betweens, #8 or #9) if you plan to hand quilt. A sharp nee dle with an eye large enough for sportweight yarn is necessary you plan to tie a comforter.

Pins

Multi-colored glass or plastic headed pins are generally longe stronger and easier to see and hold than regular dressmaker pins.

Thimble

Protection for your middle finger is necessary when quiltir There are different thimble styles. Purchase one that fits your m dle finger comfortably and has well defined indentations. Wea whenever stitching so it will feel natural when quilting.

Iron and Ironing Board

A shot of steam is useful.

74

Marking Devices

Most marking can be done with a regular #2 lead pencil and a white dressmaker's pencil. Keep them sharp. There is a blue felt tip marking pen available that is water erasable; it works especially well for marking quilting designs. (When you no longer need the lines for guides, dab them with cool water and the blue marks will disappear.) Ask the salespeople at your local fabric or quilt shop about marking pens. There are several different kinds on the market.

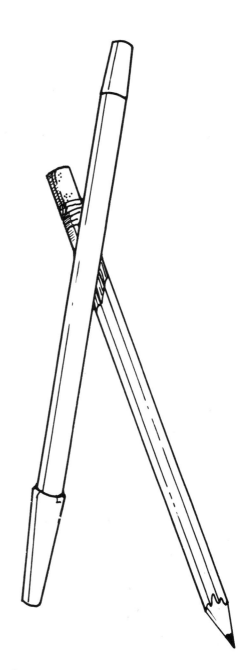

Materials

Batting

Batting is the filler in a quilt or comforter. Thick batting is used in comforters that are tied. A piece of bonded polyester batting from a roll (5- or 6-ounce weight) is fine. Check at your local quilt or fabric store for batting, and read the labels for size and thickness.

Special thick polyester batting is available for comforters. This batting is made for tying or commercial machine quilting and is very difficult to quilt by hand.

You need thin batting for hand quilting. Thin batting comes in 100% polyester, 100% cotton and a cotton-polyester (80-20%) combination. I recommend Mountain Mist® batting manufactured by the Stearns and Foster Company.

A 100% cotton batting requires close quilting to prevent shifting and separating in the wash. Most old quilts have cotton batting and are rather flat. Cotton is a good natural fiber that lasts well and is compatible with cotton and cotton blend fabrics.

A 100% polyester batting requires much less quilting. If batting is glazed or bonded, it is easy to work with, won't pull apart and has more loft than cotton batting.

Needlepunch

Unbonded polyester or needlepunch is the type of batting used in strip quilting. Although it has a lower loft than other battings, your projects will have a soft, puffy look. I recommend needlepunch because of its stability and ease of sewing. It is difficult to sew the strips together accurately on top of high-loft batting. Needlepunch does not require a foundation or base fabric underneath it in order to be machine sewn.

Threads

For machine piecing, use white or neutral thread as light in color as your lightest fabric. Use a dark neutral thread for piecing dark solids. It is easier to work with 100% cotton thread on some machines.

For hand quilting, use special quilting thread or wax regular thread. Sportweight yarn or pearl cotton is good for tying comforters.

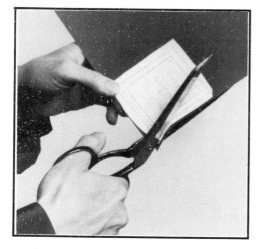

Making a stiffened template

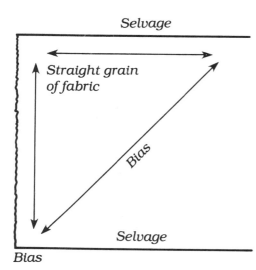

Bias

Bias

Using a paper template

Techniques

After the quilt design has been chosen, colors planned, a materials gathered together, the business of cutting and sewing gins. Quiltmaking is a craft that requires close attention, accura and patience. It is both relaxing and practical.

For me, there is great joy in watching my quilt designs grow a sew. The work is fun and will progress smoothly if you are care and precise about it from the very beginning.

Templates

In patchwork, pattern pieces are called templates. After decidi on a design and fabrics, the next step is to make templates. Caref ly trace the templates from the book onto graph paper or traci paper. Trace accurately and transfer to the paper all informati printed on the template in the book.

There are two ways to use these templates: use them as pap patterns to cut around, or use them stiffened to trace around befc you cut. Paper templates are simply cut out and used. To make s fened templates, roughly cut out the pattern pieces (outside t cutting line). Glue each one to a thin piece of plastic (x-ray film good) or lightweight posterboard. Cut out the paper pattern and stiffening together. Be precise. Make a template for each shape the design.

Cutting

Study the design and templates. Determine the number of piec to cut of each shape and each fabric. Trim off the selvage before yc begin cutting. When one fabric is to be used both for borders and the unit block designs, cut the borders first and the smaller piec from what is left over.

At the ironing board, press and fold the fabric so that one, two four layers can be cut at one time (except for linear prints li stripes and checks that should be cut one at a time). Fold the fabr so that each piece will be cut on the straight of grain.

When using a stiffened template, position it on the fabric so tl arrows match the straight grain of fabric. With a sharp penc (white for dark fabrics, lead for light ones) trace around tl template on the fabric. This is the cutting line. Cut just inside th line to most accurately duplicate the template.

For a paper template, line it up with the straight grain of fabri Hold it in place on the fabric and cut around it. Be precise. Compa cut pieces with the template to be sure they are true.

In machine piecing there are no drawn lines to guide your se ing. The seamline is 1/4" from the cut edge of the fabric so this ou side edge must be precisely cut to ensure accurate sewing.

After cutting the necessary number of pieces of each color a shape for one unit block, arrange the pieces on a flat surface in t desired design. This will help you determine which pieces to s together first and evaluate your fabric choices and arrangeme Always make one sample block of a design before embarking o large project.

Machine Piecing

Sew exact 1/4" seams. To determine the 1/4" seam allowance on your machine, place a template under the presser foot and gently lower the needle onto the seamline. The distance from the needle to the edge of the template is 1/4". Lay a piece of masking tape at the edge of the template to act as the 1/4" guide. If the presser foot edge is at the 1/4" mark, use the edge as a guide. Stitch length should be set at 10-12 stitches per inch. For most of the sewing in this book, sew from cut edge to cut edge (exceptions will be noted). Backtack if you wish, although it is not really necessary as each seam will be crossed and held by another.

Use chain piecing whenever possible to save time and thread. To chain piece, sew one seam, but do not lift the presser foot. Do not take the piece out of the sewing machine, and do not cut the thread. Instead, set up the next seam to be sewn and stitch it as you did the first. There will be a little twist of thread between the two pieces. Sew all the seams you can at one time in this way, then remove the "chain." Clip the threads.

Press the seam allowances to one side, toward the darker fabric when possible. Avoid too much ironing as you sew because it tends to stretch biases and distort fabric shapes.

To piece a unit block, sew the smallest pieces together first to form units. Join smaller units to form larger ones until the block is complete. Pay close attention to the design drawing and sewing instructions given with the patterns.

Short seams need not be pinned unless there is matching involved, or the seam is longer than 4". Keep pins away from the seamline. Sewing over pins tends to burr the needle and makes it hard to be accurate in tight places.

Ideally, if pieces are cut and sewn precisely, patchwork designs will come out flat and smooth with crisply matched corners and points. In practice, it doesn't always happen that way. Here are four matching techniques that can be helpful in many different piecing situations.

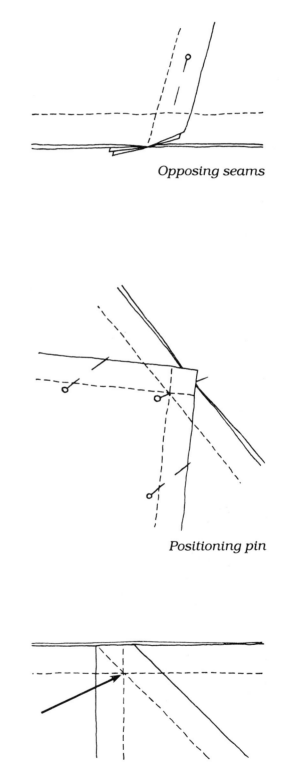

Opposing seams

Positioning pin

- Opposing Seams: When stitching one seamed unit to another, press seam allowances on the seams that need to match in opposite directions. The two "opposing" seams will hold each other in place and evenly distribute the bulk. Plan your pressing to take advantage of opposing seams.

Positioning Pin: A pin carefully pushed straight through two points, that need to match, and pulled tight will establish the proper point of matching. Pin the seam normally and remove the positioning pin before stitching.

The "X": When triangles are pieced, stitches will form an "X" at the next seamline. Stitch through the center of the "X" to make sure the points on the sewn triangles will not be chopped off.

Easing: When two pieces to be sewn together are supposed to match but instead are slightly different lengths, pin the points of matching, and stitch with the shorter piece on top. The feed dogs will ease the fullness of the bottom piece.

You can do beautiful and accurate piecing on the sewing machine. Try to correct mistakes when they happen (keep a seam ripper handy), but don't spend too much time ripping out and resewing. Some sewing inaccuracies are correctable, some are not. Sometimes the best thing is to move on and make the next block better. The quality of your piecing will improve as you go along.

The "X"

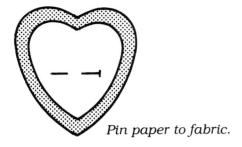

Pin paper to fabric.

Baste fabric to paper, sewing through paper.

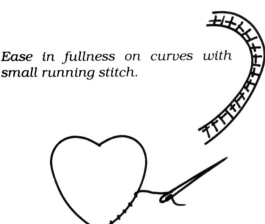

Ease in fullness on curves with small running stitch.

Blind stitch fabric to background.

House Stencil:

Paper Patch Applique

Applique is used on several of the quilts and projects in this book. You may applique by hand or machine. I prefer using a technique called Paper Patch Applique.

1. Make templates for all pattern pieces from medium weight bond paper. Do not add seam allowance.
2. Place templates on fabric and draw 1/4" from all edges of template with an appropriate marking device.
3. Cut all fabric pieces along the drawn line.
4. Pin fabric to template.
5. Fold 1/4" seam allowances over template. Baste fabric to template, using a running stitch and sewing through the paper.
6. Clip inner curves and indentations, gently stretching fabric.
7. On outer curves, ease in fullness, using a small running stitch to gather the fabric. Do not sew through paper on outer curves. The basting stitches that go through the paper on either end of the outer curve will hold the fabric to the paper.
8. Baste all fabric pieces to paper. Do not use a knot after the last basting stitches since the basting stitches and paper must be removed in a later step.
9. Press all fabric pieces, easing fabric to ensure that bumpy edges are not created during pressing.
10. Applique fabric pieces to background, using a small blind stitch and matching thread. Stitches should be fairly close together. When applique of each piece is almost complete, pull basting thread from fabric and remove paper from the small opening that remains. A pair of tweezers is helpful for this step. If you completed the applique and forgot to remove the paper, make a small slit through the back side of the background fabric and remove paper with tweezers.

Quick Stencil Pattern:

If you will be using your stencil only one time, you may want t make these quick stencils.

Cut out the shape of motif. Place the motif on adhesive-backe paper and trace around the shape with a dark pencil or pen. Usin scissors or a craft knife, cut out the motif.

Remove the protective backing from the adhesive paper. Pre the adhesive paper onto the fabric to be stenciled, centering th design. Smooth evenly onto the fabric, making sure there are wrinkles.

When stenciling has been completed, remove the adhesiv backed paper and discard.

Stenciling Fabric:

Tape a piece of fabric, cut to the proper size and shape for the dividual project, right-side-up, on a flat work surface. Center st cil, tacky-side-down, on fabric. Smooth all motif edges.

Follow manufacturer's directions on stencil paint to stencil. dry completely before using fabric stencil motif in project. Pr with hot iron (350°) to heat set paint.

The Quilt Top

Setting the Quilt Together

When all of the blocks are pieced, you are ready to "set" the quilt top together, following a setting plan. First stitch together blocks or blocks and lattices into rows, using 1/4" seams. Then stitch together rows of blocks or rows of blocks and lattice strips. Setting sequences are shown in diagrams.

When the center portion is pieced together, borders may then be added to the quilt.

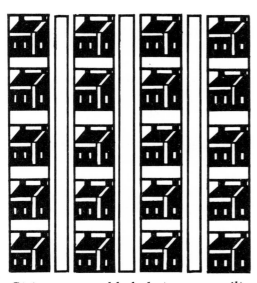

Strips are added between quilt blocks. Long pieces of lattice are then pieced to columns of blocks and lattice.

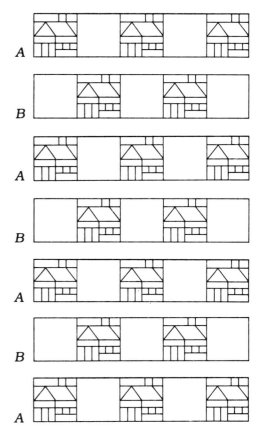

Alternate blocks are joined in rows; rows are then joined together.

Lattice squares are pieced to lattice. Lattice strips are pieced around quilt blocks. Join rows of lattice strips and squares to rows of quilt blocks and lattice.

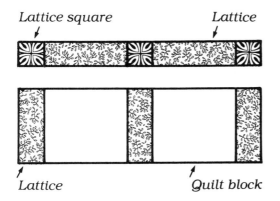

Lattice square　　*Lattice*

Lattice　　*Quilt block*

Borders

Borders function as a frame to a quilt design. Each of the quilt designs in this book has directions for one type of border treatment. You can make a different border than the one shown. Simply find the border treatment that you prefer on a different quilt and use those border directions on the quilt you're making (adjusting measurements if necessary). You will find simple borders with straight sewn corners, single striped or multiple plain borders with mitered corners, and more elaborate pieced borders.

For plain borders with straight sewn corners, first sew borders to the long side of the quilt, then to the width. Striped fabrics make lovely quilt borders, but the corners must be mitered to make the design turn the corner gracefully. Mitered corners are not difficult to do and are worth the effort in some design situations. Miter corners when using stripes or multiple plain borders.

You will need to buy fabric the length of the longest outside border plus about 4" to allow for shrinkage. It is often wise when cutting border strips to leave them 3" or 4" longer than the length given in the pattern. When the actual dimensions of the quilt top are known, the border strips can be trimmed to fit.

Border strips should always be cut from yardage before the templates, ensuring that you have continuous yardage. If you need to piece border strips, seams should be pressed open and placed in the center of each side of the quilt for minimum visibility. If you are using a striped border, it is best not to piece it.

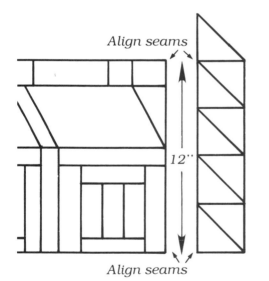

Align seams

12"

Align seams

3" Sawtooth border segments

Pieced Borders

Pieced borders frame several of the quilts in this book. The Sawtooth border is found on the Schoolhouse quilt shown in Plate 15 on page 47, Comforts of Home Quilt shown in Plate 5 on page 43, and the School House quilt in Plate 12 on page 45. An elaborate border of strip pieced trees encloses both houses and trees in Cabin in the Country shown in Plate 11 on page 45.

Pattern pieces have been given for all pieced borders. Use the diagram accompanying each quilt to help determine placement of border pieces. Be sure to measure the border segments as you piece, keeping them the exact size. A slight variation in border segment size will cause the border strip to vary greatly from the quilt top, since there are so many border segments in the border strip.

Each border has been designed so there are a certain number of border segments per quilt block. Be sure to piece border strips to quilt with seams aligned.

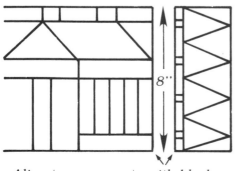

8"

Align tree segments with blocks

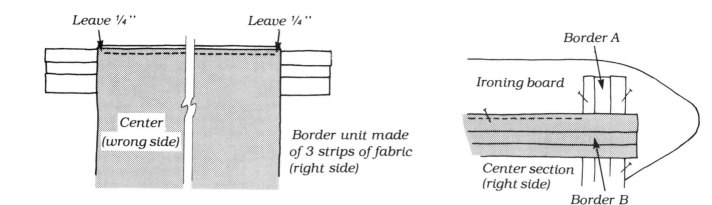

Leave ¼" *Leave ¼"*

Center (wrong side)

Border unit made of 3 strips of fabric (right side)

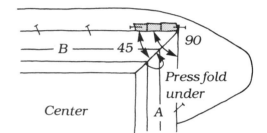

Border A

Ironing board

Center section (right side)

Border B

Mitering

1. Prepare the borders. Determine the finished outside dimensions of the quilt. Cut the borders this length plus 1/2" for seam allowances. When using a striped fabric for the borders, make sure the design on all four borders is cut the same way. Multiple borders should be sewn together and the resulting "striped" units treated as a single border for mitering.

2. To attach the border to the pieced section of the quilt, center each border on a side so the ends extend equally on either side of the center section. Using a 1/4" seam allowance, sew the border to the center, leaving 1/4" unsewn at the beginning and end of the stitching line. Press the seam allowances toward the border.

. Arrange the first corner to be mitered on the ironing board as illustrated. Press the corner flat and straight. To prevent it from slipping, pin the quilt to the ironing board. Following the illustration, turn border "B" right side up, folding the corner to be mitered under at a 45° angle. Match the raw edges underneath with those of border "A." Fuss with it until it looks good. The stripes and border designs should meet. Check the squareness of the corner with a right angle. Press the fold. This will be the sewing line. Pin the borders together to prevent shifting and unpin the piece from the board. Turn wrong side out and pin along the fold line, readjusting if necessary to match the designs.

Machine baste from the inside to the outside corner on the fold line, leaving 1/4" at the beginning unsewn. Check for accuracy. If it is right, sew again with a regular stitch. Backtack at the beginning and end of the stitching line. (After you have mitered several times, the basting step ceases to be necessary.) Trim the excess fabric to 1/4" along the mitered seam. Press this seam open. Press the other seams to the outside.

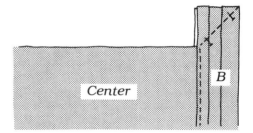

B — *45* — *90*

Press fold under

Center *A*

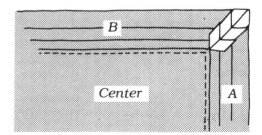

Center *B*

B

Center *A*

Finishing

Once a quilt top is pieced and has borders, there are two ways to finish it. It can be quilted or tied. Quilt with a thin batting and backing by hand or machine. Tie with a thick batting and backing to make a fluffy comforter. The method you choose will depend upon how the quilt is to be used and how much time you have to put into it. Hand quilting is the nicest way to finish a quilt, but it takes a long time. Machine quilting is strong and functional, takes less time, but is less attractive. Tying does the job and is very quick.

Vine quilting design[12]

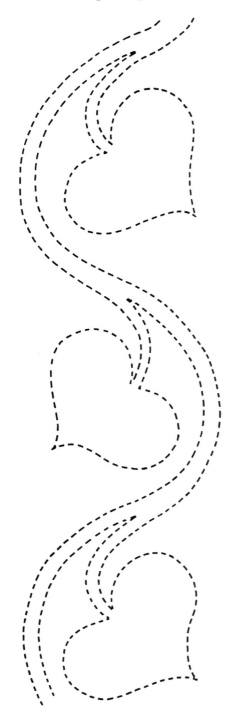

Preparing to Quilt

Quilting can be done by hand or machine. The preparation for each is the same.

1. Press the quilt top. Lightly mark the quilting lines using a blue water-erasable pen, a white marking pencil, or a #2 lead pencil. Where you place the quilting lines will depend upon the quilt top design, the type of batting you are using and how much quilting you want to do. There are many pretty, traditional quilting motifs that fit nicely in plain spaces such as unpieced blocks and borders. Quilt supply stores carry stencils for these designs which are quite easy to use. If you do not wish to quilt hearts, flowers and feathered wreaths, mark the quilt top with an allover design such as a grid of squares or diamonds, or parallel diagonal lines. Or, you can plan to quilt 1/4" away on each side of every seamline, for which no marking is necessary. Quilting suggestions have been included with each quilt design. Try to avoid quilting too close to the seamlines as the bulk of the seam allowances might slow you down. Also keep in mind that the purpose of quilting, besides its esthetic value, is to securely hold the three layers of the quilt together. Do not leave large spaces unquilted.

2. Prepare the backing. If a quilt or wall hanging is less than 42" wide, simply measure the length of the quilt and purchase yardage in that amount. If a quilt or wall hanging is more than 42" wide, you will need to piece the backing. Purchase twice the quilt width and seam together. Cut the backing 1" larger all the way around than the quilt top. Press thoroughly with the seams open. Lay the backing face down on a large, flat, clean surface. Using masking tape, tape the backing down (without stretching) to keep it smooth and flat while you are working with the other layers.

3. Cut the batting the same size as the backing and lay it on top. Smooth it out as well as you can.

4. Center the freshly ironed and marked quilt top face up on top of the batting. Starting in the middle, pin baste the three layers together while gently smoothing the fullness to the sides and corners as you go. After pinning, baste the layers together with needle and light colored thread. Start in the center and make radiating lines of stitches. After basting, remove the pins. Now you are ready to quilt.

12. *Quilting design from Shirley Thompson,* **The Finishing Touch**, *Powell Publications, P.O. Box 513, Edmonds, Washington 98020.*

Hand Quilting

To quilt by hand, you will need quilting thread, quilting needles, small scissors, a thimble, and maybe a balloon or large rubber band to help grasp the needle if it gets stuck. Quilt on a frame, a large hoop, or just on a table or your lap. Use a single thread no longer than 18''. Make a small, single knot in the end of the thread. The quilting stitch is a small, running stitch that goes through all three layers of the quilt. To begin, insert the needle in the top layer about 3/4'' from the point you want to start stitching. Pull the needle out at the starting point and gently tug at the knot until it pops through the fabric and is buried in the batting. Make a small backstitch through all three layers at the beginning of the quilting line. Proceed to quilt with small, even stitches until coming almost to the end of the thread. There, make a single knot fairly close to the fabric. Make a backstitch to bury the knot in the batting. Run the thread off through the batting and out the quilt top, and snip it off. Repeat until the whole quilt is quilted.

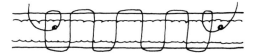

Hand quilting stitch

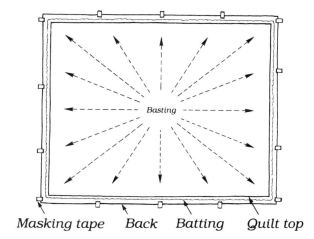

Basting

Masking tape   *Back*   *Batting*   *Quilt top*

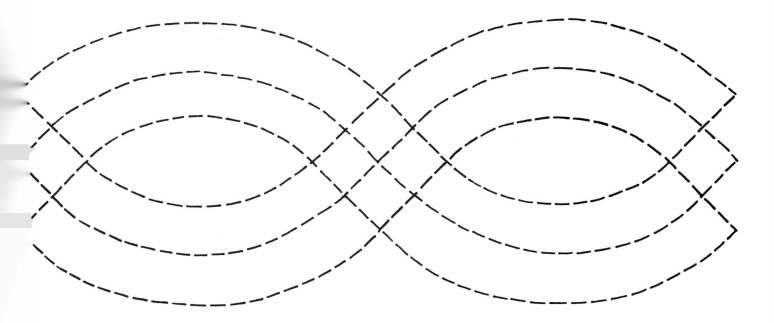

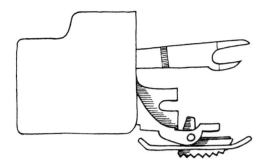

Machine Quilting

Small quilts can be quilted on some home sewing machines without much trouble. Plan and mark a simple straight-line quilting design such as a grid or parallel diagonal lines. Use regular thread that won't show too much. Many machines have a special attachment for sewing through several layers. Check with your sewing machine dealer to see what is available for your machine. It is well worth the trouble. A regular sewing presser foot pushes the top layer of fabric along faster than the ones beneath, and tends to pucker and pleat the piece as you sew. An "even-feed" or "walking" foot feeds all three layers smoothly and evenly.

Machine quilting can be somewhat of a struggle. Try not to rush and it will be finished before you know it. Plan simple straight quilting lines that extend across the piece, from edge to edge. Start near the center of the quilt and work toward the edges. The part of the quilt not being worked on tends to be bulky and gets in the way. To help handle it, clear a large space on your sewing table to support the weight. Make a neat roll of the part of the quilt that needs to fit under the sewing machine arm. Carefully stitch on the marked quilting lines until the whole piece is quilted.

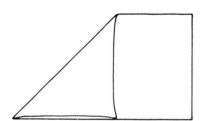

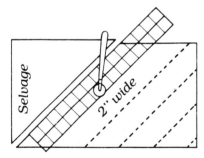

Marking bias strips

Binding

After quilting, trim the excess batting and backing to the edge of the quilt front. Finish the raw edges with bias binding. Bias binding can be purchased by the package or yard, or you can make it from a 3/4 yard piece of fabric.

Make your own bias binding by folding over a corner of fabric to find the true bias. Make a crease at the fold. Open the fold and cut along the crease. Measure 2"-wide strips and mark with a pencil. Cut the strips. A clear plastic ruler and rotary cutter are especially helpful for cutting bias strips. With right sides together, machine stitch the bias strip ends in 1/4" seams. Press the seams open and trim away excess seam edges. To make a double-fold bias strip, press a crease down the center of the strip. Open the fabric so that it is flat, with the wrong side facing up. Fold the raw edges to the crease line. Press. Fold in half along the original crease line. Press again.

Joining bias strips

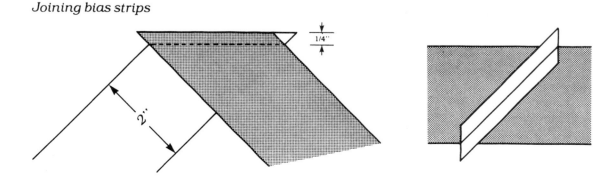

Bibliography

Bacon, Lenice Ingram, *American Patchwork Quilts.* New York: Bonanza Books, 1973.

Beyer, Jinny, *Patchwork Patterns.* McLean, Virginia: EPM Publications, Inc., 1979.

Holstein, Jonathan, *The Pieced Quilt.* Boston: New York Graphic Society, 1973.

Holstein, Jonathan, and John Finley, *Kentucky Quilts.* Louisville, Kentucky: The Kentucky Quilt Project, Inc., 1982.

Martin, Judy, *Patchworkbook.* New York: Charles Scribner's Sons, 1983.

McCloskey, Marsha, *Small Quilts.* Bothell, Washington: That Patchwork Place, Inc., 1982.

McCloskey, Marsha, *Wall Quilts.* New York: Dover Publications, Inc., 1983, 1990.

McKim, Ruby, *101 Patchwork Patterns.* New York: Dover Publications, Inc., 1962.

Nelson, Cyril I., *The Quilt Engagement Calendar 1984.* New York: E.P. Dutton, Inc., 1983.

Nelson, Cyril I., *The Quilt Engagement Calendar 1983.* New York: E.P. Dutton, Inc., 1982.

Nelson, Cyril I., *The Quilt Engagement Calendar 1982.* New York: E.P. Dutton, Inc., 1981.

Patterson, Jane M., "The Little Red Schoolhouse: Morning, Noon, and Night," *Quilters Newsletter Magazine,* (September, 1983).

Quilts, A Tradition of Variations. Albany, California: East Bay Heritage Quilters, 1982.

Safford, Carleton L. and Robert Bishop, *America's Quilts and Coverlets.* New York: Weathervane Books, 1974.

Thompson, Shirley, *The Finishing Touch.* Edmonds, Washington: Powell Publications, 1980.

Walker, Michele, *The Pattern Library Quilting and Patchwork.* New York: Ballantine Books, 1983.

Metric Conversion Chart

1/4"	=	6mm
1/2"	=	13mm
5/8"	=	16mm
1"	=	2.5 cm
1/8 yd.	=	12 cm
1/4 yd.	=	23 cm
3/8 yd.	=	35 cm
1/2 yd.	=	45 cm
5/8 yd.	=	60 cm
3/4 yd.	=	75 cm
1 yd.	=	91.5 cm
1 1/2 yds.	=	1.38 m
2 yds.	=	1.83 m

Biographical Information

Nancy J. Martin, a former teacher, utilizes her background in education to teach and encourage quilters of all levels. She is recognized internationally for her designs, classes and lectures.

Nancy is president of That Patchwork Place, Inc., and author of several quilting books: *Houses, Cottages and Cabins Patchwork Quilts: With Full-Size Patterns*, *Pieces of the Past*, *Back to Square One*, *A Banner Year* and *Threads of Time*. Nancy wrote *A Dozen Variables* and *Ocean Waves* with coauthor Marsha McCloskey. She has also produced a video, *Shortcuts to America's Best-Loved Quilts*, which focuses on the Bias Square™ ruler that she developed and the techniques for using it.

Nancy is active in her local quilt guild and is a member of the American Quilt Study Group and the American International Quilt Association.